THE FUTURE OF DECLINE

T0315522

# THE FUTURE OF DECLINE

*Anglo-American Culture at Its Limits*

JED ESTY

**stanford briefs**
An Imprint of Stanford University Press
Stanford, California

Stanford University Press
Stanford, California

Printed in the United States of America on acid-free, archival-quality paper

ISBN 9781503633315 (paper)
ISBN 9781503633674 (ebook)
Library of Congress Control Number 2022935899
CIP data available upon request.

Cover image: from the National Air and Space Museum Space Suit Collection, X-Ray Photography, by permission of NASM.

Cover design: Rob Ehle

Typeset by Classic Typography in 11/15 Adobe Garamond

# CONTENTS

# PREFACE: LOST GREATNESS AS A WAY OF LIFE

In August 2008, Americans watched the Beijing Olympics opening ceremony, marveling at Zhang Yimou's spectacle of a newly confident, abundantly creative nation. Commentaries popped up all over the US media, noting that the impeccable organization, the daring aesthetics, the avant-garde architecture, and the massive scale of project management in Beijing heralded the arrival of a new Asian superpower. A month later, Lehman Brothers fell and tipped the world into financial crisis.

By the time 2012 rolled around, an economic recovery had been engineered in the US with the indispensable aid of Chinese capital. Over in London, the Olympics kicked off again, this time with an opening ceremony masterminded by Danny Boyle. Boyle's films, *Shallow Grave* and *Trainspotting* as well as *Slumdog Millionaire* and *Steve Jobs*, tell stories of cold poverty in the UK, hot wealth in the colonies. His "Isles of Wonder" show seemed forced even on the spot. It confused spectators.

Flashes of imperial glory jangled against dashes of social-welfare pragmatism. Dancing health-care workers as a global sign of Britishness? The grandiloquent blend of past and present, with its hipster revisionism and blenderized ideologies, seemed to signify everything at once about the UK and therefore nothing at all. It highlighted the UK's unfinished business of reckoning with an imperial past and a European future.

Beijing 2008 and London 2012 struck a nerve for American viewers. The rising superpower across the Pacific and the fading empire across the Atlantic seemed to sandwich an American Century on the wane. The glamorous techno-futurism of Beijing and the zombie wax-museum antics of London threw America's uncertain fate into relief. With Wall Street so recently in free fall, the US media was divided between faltering belief in national power and swaggering insistence on American greatness.

For those of us who came of age in the 1970s, the two Olympic ceremonies simply rekindled what I suspect was a familiar sense of diminished expectations. For Generation X, political awareness began with Vietnam and Watergate. After the end of the gold standard, the oil crisis, stagflation, the drug wars, and the crime waves, the 1970s ended with the Iran hostage crisis and Carter's so-called national malaise speech. Where young Baby Boomers saw American greatness embodied in the Apollo missions, we saw the fiery failure of the Challenger crash in 1986. The 1980s and 1990s—the time of our youth—featured a strange subterranean battle between the slow steady ebb of national confidence and the resurgent rhetoric of "Morning in America," victory in the Cold War, and the tech boom. Those signifiers of American renewal often seemed stagey and brittle, more bravado than strength. Twilight and morning, autumn and apex: for my generation, the rhetoric of American destiny felt like a game of bad metaphors, a partisan opera played over a deep bass note of loss.

The twin crises of the Bush II era therefore hit like a return to the norm of national decline. 9/11 revealed the fragility of American security. The subprime crisis revealed the fragility of American prosperity. Both brought back familiar anxieties of a tottering superpower. They marked an Islamophobic and Sinophobic reboot of aggressive political sentiments that had already been aimed at Russia in my childhood, Japan in my youth.

As a graduate student and young scholar, I spent the last half of the 1990s studying literary culture in the UK's age of imperial contraction. Looking back now, I can see that my research was a refracted and delayed investigation into a problem closer to home: American decline. It was also an intellectual evasion of the racial and colonial problems underlying American supremacy. Back then, I wanted to know if Great Writing in English—the ability to capture whole worlds in a novel or a poem—depended on Britain's status as a Great Power. My research eventually took the form of a book somewhat misleadingly entitled *A Shrinking Island*. What it suggested was that British contraction produced a number of effects, not all of them negative, nativist, or scarcity-driven. The era of decolonization, of modernizing sex and gender norms, and of the Keynesian welfare state represented a step forward for many in the UK. Imperial contraction was not pure loss. Nor did the shrinking of the British domain translate into social backwardness. It was part of a modernization process, not a tumble back through time. To cede the pretensions of global hegemony—then or now—is not to regress or decline, except in the minds of those in thrall to superpower nostalgia.

The optimistic idea driving this book is similar: the US can move forward while its power wanes. The questions that faced the UK on its historical downslope face the US now. Can the waning of global power reinvigorate domestic society? Will post-peak America be even more divided? Can a culture of contraction inspire citizens to find an inclusive, egalitarian, contemporary sense of national purpose? The Trump-Brexit era has dramatized with remarkable immediacy the doubt embedded in such questions. The questions are not new, but they are more urgent as America becomes—any day now—a second-place nation. The answers will redefine US culture and society in the decades ahead.

*The Future of Decline* is a short study of a long American twilight, informed by British precedent. The undisputed peak of US power started in 1945, and its fade began in the 1970s. Americans have now been on the downslope for almost a generation longer than they were at the superpower summit. And the UK, which was a global hegemon from the end of the Napoleonic wars (1815) through to World War I (1914) has now been, by that time line, in decline for more than a hundred years.

Decline, in other words, lasts a long time. Empires fall dramatically in our lore, but hegemony dies slowly in fact. And declin*ism*—the rhetoric of once and future greatness—lasts even longer. One hundred years of ebbing force in the UK have not stilled its lingering dreams of glory. Can the US escape that fate, or will the morbid symptoms of declinist thinking—MAGA and melancholia—stay with us for the long haul ahead? In America, declinism is practically a way of life, a cultural birthright, from the Puritan Jeremiad to the paranoid hegemony of the Cold War, from the lost City on a Hill to the closing frontier of F. J. Turner, from Sputnik to Watergate, from oil crisis to climate emergency, from the subprime crash to the Covid-19 pandemic.

As this book goes to press, the perennial dark fantasy of American declinism is converging with a new structural reality. By most projections, the 2020s will be the last decade when the US economy is the largest in the world. China already leads the world in so-called purchasing power parity—one leading indicator of national wealth. Countless books about the American eclipse will quickly follow, glutting an already saturated market. Whether left-leaning or right-leaning, fatalistic or optimistic, such books share certain features. First, mainstream declinist writing in the US—dominated by economists, journalists, and political scientists—tends to battle over metrics and statistics while ignoring the decisive story lines that shape most Americans' perception of decline. Second, such writing tends to filter decline anxieties through an elite worldview. Declinism in most of its forms overidentifies with elite fears of lost power and position. It underidentifies with nonwhite, nonmale, nonpropertied citizens. Third, the prophets and pundits of US decline too often use the specters of fallen Rome and shrunken Britain to shake rather than inform readers.

By contrast, this book uses UK history to advance the idea that the loss of national greatness is neither quick nor catastrophic, neither tragic nor avoidable. The UK experience provides suggestive examples—and counterexamples—for US citizens hoping to live good, meaningful lives in an ex-superpower. Rather than evoke British imperialism as a spectacle of diminishment, it considers UK history since Suez as a story about the struggle for unevenly distributed resources. British decline forced UK citizens to try to redefine their national identity without the governing narratives of crown and empire at the forefront. Brexit shows how far from complete that process is (Barnett, O'Toole, Ward and Rasch). But it is a cultural process, not shackled to the iron laws of global trade. An ex-hegemon can become something other than a shadow of its former self. In the coming decades, Americans will need to relinquish Cold War certainties about American power in order to reinvent the shared meaning of US society.

For now, the narcissistic goad of "lost greatness" still resonates for many Americans, and not just right-wing patriots. It will resonate even after the memory of Trump's gross demagoguery fades. It resonates because there is a wide, bipartisan, and popular desire to stay on top after four decades of fading economic supremacy.

Most of all, it resonates because Americans do not have access to a galvanizing alternative language for a common national purpose. It is time to shelve the old habituated language of US dominance, to face the multipolar world of the future, to tell new American stories. To find and circulate those stories is a difficult but necessary task. They will have to be vivid and visceral, dense with real US history, ripe for collective affiliation. They will have to make multiracial democracy and social welfare compatible with the lived experiences and popular culture of most Americans—not some, not half. That is a serious project for media, political, and academic elites—for cultural gatekeepers and knowledge workers of all kinds. To advance it, the traditional center must cede the language of US supremacy, and the progressive left must cede the language of anti-nationalism. America has to represent something more than global supremacy now. Eternal superpower status is a fantasy and—even were it true—it is a broadly anti-democratic desire, at odds with the nation's egalitarian ideals.

Conservative declinism blocks both the liberal goal of incremental progress and the progressive goal of social transformation. It tells its anxious adherents that America was once more truly itself than it is now. That is nonsense. America in 2020 is no less (nor more) America than it was in 1950. Heroic narratives of endless growth now obscure rather than reveal the meaning of America. We can no longer just light out for the frontier. The nation is no Huck Finn today, if it ever was. And even Huck was no innocent.

Rather than ape the nostalgia of the British governing classes over the long imperial twilight, US citizens might prefer—however much they are invested in social hierarchy—to abandon morbid and melancholy delusions. They might prefer to see the US as a decent society rather than a diminished hegemon. The American future need not repeat the Brexit present—a nation holding fast to its glory days like an aging quarterback. That's a geopolitical sequel nobody wants to see. The loss of the hegemonic top slot is an economic given. But the culture and politics of the response is not. What has a pressing claim on American attention now is the story of British adaptation to loss, not the spectacle of the loss itself.

Yet declinism almost always sells as part of the epic historical cycle of imperial rise-and-fall. That mesmerizing epic is, in a way, the subtext of almost all modern historical thinking, from Edward Gibbon's *The History of the Decline and Fall of the Roman Empire* to *Sid Meier's Civilization VI*. It has served as the subtext and context for almost every consequential discussion of arts, politics, economics, ideas, and social institutions in the US since 1975. The welter of fading-hegemony literature feeds a national fascination with how fast and far we will fall, or—for the hopeful—how long America will hold on to solo superpower status. Both sides—the tragic and the magic—obscure a fundamental question: What does decline *mean*? What is the significance, in experiential and everyday terms—in feelings and fantasies as well as in metrics and policies—of living in a country past its prime? We know plenty about rising and falling empires.

But we have a fundamental—and bipartisan—deficit in our imaginative understanding of life after hegemony.

America is old enough now to have two archives telling the story of its destiny. One existed *before* it was a global power (but still a juggernaut of continental and colonial expansion). One came into being *while* it was a global power, in the twentieth century. At this new turning point in history, a third archive is beginning to emerge. What trajectories can we glimpse for an American future *after* its apex as a global power—even, perhaps, after Americans have acknowledged and adjusted to the downslope of history? In an effort to detach the national gaze from lost greatness, this book pursues four interlocking projects: (1) a critical overview of US declinism since 2000, outlining its bugs and features; (2) a list of ten theses for describing the future of decline without the pervasive drag of superpower nostalgia; (3) a comparative analysis of British and American thinking about national identity after global supremacy; and (4) a map of emerging narratives about American history and American destiny for the age of limits.

Growing up in the 1970s, I took in a steady stream of declinist images and narratives. By contrast, I believe that my grandparents, coming of age in the 1920s, saw the US as a nation on the rise and that my parents, coming of age in the 1950s, saw the US as a secure superpower. As this book goes to press in 2022, I'm not sure my children believe in a meaningful American future. Four generations, one arc: from upswing to peak to downslope to crisis. America's season of global supremacy set the horizon of expectation for the Greatest Generation and the Baby Boomers. Even as they recede into historical haze, those expectations still define the outer limit of the public discourse. Few leaders or politicians will demur when asked if the US is the greatest country now, the greatest country ever. But the boomers are aging fast and the world is changing even faster. The old reflex to declare US greatness will stop twitching at some point, maybe sooner than we think.

Belief in US national superiority lives inside almost all the ordinary and available languages of American patriotism. It took a long time to build up this rigid version of nationalist feeling, and it will take a conscious effort to shed it. Belief in natural superiority was made in America—the military-industrial complex's most successful product. It can be unmade, too, without destroying patriotic sentiment, without losing wealth and security, without ceding the idea of robust citizenship. It can be unmade unless the rhetoric of greatness stays lodged in the American mind, too sacred to be dispatched by the light and logic of history on the downslope.

THE FUTURE OF DECLINE

# 1 AGAINST DECLINISM

Decline is a fact; *declinism* is a problem. American decline is happening, slowly but inevitably. It is a structural and material process. Declinism is a problem of rhetoric or belief. This book is about the cultural causes and material consequences of certain predominant strains of declinism. In particular, this chapter is about the contradictions built in to the massive and growing literature on American decline. Declinism is a widely shared script about American public life in which lost power is the core assumption. I take the term *declinism* to describe the entire body of writing and thinking built on that assumption, including both its alarmist and its optimistic poles. Both the alarmism and the optimism perpetuate the shopworn idea that supremacy, lost or regained, is the most important quality about the US.

Declinism is the way that media elites predict the future of an aging superpower for its educated public. For two generations now, economists, historians, and

journalists have eyed the spectacle of American descent
(Luce). Countless books and magazine articles land with
a gloomy thud, testifying to America's narrowing horizons. Like nervous senators in the days of Nero, declinists seem ready to hail glory or cry doom as the political
winds and market indices shift. No wonder that citizens
and readers become alert to twitches in stock markets
and gas prices, but blind to capitalism's long-term and
ecological limits. Readers are too often left with a set of
moralized narratives or how-to manuals about how to
recognize or reverse the loss of superpower status. The
true slow fade of American power is our national open
secret, resting somewhere between a profane taboo and a
banal truism. Forsworn by public leaders and feared by
an edgy public, the end of the American Century is
almost constantly conjured and banished in churning
cycles of incoherent thinking.

Contemporary declinism builds on a centuries-long
tradition of the American jeremiad, a genre of prophetic
dissent and moral warning about national decadence
(Jendrysik). It hit a decisive phase and took on its contemporary form in the 1970s. At that time, the bipolar
model of the Cold War still prevailed. Declinism toggled
between the malaise of the 1970s and the bravado of the
1980s. The 1990s saw a sudden new high point for American optimism, fueled by the tech boom and what seemed
to be a unipolar world. Since 2000, declinism has grown
more alarmist again, facing a multipolar world and rapid
Chinese economic growth.

Since the 1970s, three major types of declinism have emerged. The first is what I would call Center-Left Technocratic Adjustment. It focuses on policy shifts that could mitigate or forestall the relative decline of the American economy and the eroding US position in global politics (Brzezinski, Calleo, Ikenberry, Keohane). The second is Center-Right Moral Critique. It tends to address the weakening moral fiber (work ethic, social responsibility, political will, intellectual vigor) of US culture at large. Such moral critiques—as in the work of Reaganauts Robert Bork and Bill Bennett—stoked the 1980s and 90s culture wars.[1] Technocratic and moral declinisms both exhort Americans to reverse the course of fading US supremacy. They share a can-do and how-to mentality, though the former wants to fix politics, the latter culture.

The third major type takes US decline as a complex historical event—more an inevitable fact to be accepted than a problem to be solved. Commentators of this type tend toward historical explanation rather than policy prescription. This third variant—the Big History Approach—gained traction in the 1980s, galvanized by Mancur Olson's *The Rise and Decline of Nations*, Paul Kennedy's *Rise and Fall of the Great Powers,* and Francis Fukuyama's landmark essay on the "end of history." Fukuyama's sanguine theoretical position made him the house intellectual for the unipolar dreams of a rebooted Western supremacy, in keeping with Margaret Thatcher's famous claim that there was "no alternative" to liberal, secular,

Western-style capitalist democracy. Fukuyama captured the essence of the Washington Consensus, pitching liberalized trade and low taxes as the royal road to peace and prosperity.[2]

Nineties-style triumphalism was, for all its Big History credentials, a short-horizon view of American history. Underneath the dot-com confetti and the Berlin Wall rubble, long-term relative decline continued in the US. Geopolitical and party-political divisions festered. Global trade neither erased difference nor balanced the harms of racial capitalism. Even in a decade of political confidence, the mid-1990s still featured arguments about what Samuel Huntington called the "Clash of Civilizations" and Robert Kaplan called "The Coming Anarchy." Even after the celebrated geopolitical victories that led to the unipolar 1990s, the US was losing its capacity to control the consumer desires and the electoral politics of other nations. Military superiority was not in doubt, but the dwindling force of American soft power meant that "the hegemon [was] losing its constructive powers while retaining its destructive ones" (Streeck 35). There could be no return to the Cold War peak, when hard and soft power combined with broad-gauge middle-class prosperity undergirded US hegemony. Another key work of the 1990s, Jeffrey Madrick's *The End of Affluence*, described deep cuts into American lives and dreams inflicted by stubbornly slow growth. Even with the tech sector growing, the Reagan economy calcified into a "post-welfare" society with huge wealth inequities, widespread debt, and little upward mobility. This state of affairs represented not a successful evasion of UK-style decline, but a morbid echo of Thatcherist failure.[3]

The 1990s were the pivot decade (Wegner). After 9/11, all three major types of declinism returned in force. In the last twenty years, the Center-Left Technocratic Adjustment has remained the dominant mode, issuing liberal policy prescriptions for American restoration. It picked up on the 1970s' wave of serious academic books offering diagnostic readings of America on the downslope. However pragmatic their marketing pitches, many liberal declinists evoke a rather nostalgic sense of diminishing American returns. Consider two examples, both from 2012. First, in the opening episode of Aaron Sorkin's *The Newsroom* (HBO), the protagonist Will McAvoy, played by Jeff Daniels with trademark decent-white-guy bafflement and fatigue, is asked by a student about American greatness. He responds off-script:

> We're 7th in literacy, 27th in math, 22nd in science, 49th in life expectancy, 178th in infant mortality, 3rd in median household income, number 4 in labor force and number 4 in exports. We lead the world in only three categories—number of incarcerated citizens per capita, number of adults who believe angels are real, and defense spending, where we spend more than the next 26 countries combined... So when you ask what makes us the greatest country in the world, I don't know what the fuck you're talking about.... We sure used to be...We waged wars on poverty, not poor people. We sacrificed, we cared about our neighbors, we put

our money where our mouths were, and we never beat our chest. We built great big things, made ungodly technological advances, explored the universe, cured diseases, and we cultivated the world's greatest artists and the world's greatest economy. We reached for the stars, acted like men… We were able to be all these things and do all these things because we were informed, by great men… The first step in solving any problem is recognizing there is one—America is not the greatest country in the world anymore.

The "we" of course represents elite professional white men who "acted like men," informed by "great men." With the patriarchal chain of decency, expertise, and social control broken, America is left with the hollowness of its sixty-year-old bragging rights. Liberals, too, wax nostalgic for the (white male) verities of the Eisenhower era. Second, and more soberly, is Fareed Zakaria, from his elegant book *The Post-American World*:

> The tallest building in the world is now in Dubai. The world's richest man is Mexican, and its largest publicly traded corporation is Chinese. The world's biggest plane is built in Russia and Ukraine, its leading refinery is in India, and its largest factories are all in China. By many measures, Hong Kong now rivals London and New York as the leading financial center, and the United Arab Emirates is home to the most richly endowed investment fund. Once quintessentially American icons have been appropriated by foreigners.…The biggest movie industry, in terms of both movies made and tickets sold, is Bollywood, not Hollywood.…Of the top ten malls in the world, only one is in the United

States; the world's biggest is in Dongguan, China. Such lists are arbitrary, but it is striking that twenty years ago, America was at the top in many, if not most, of these categories. (3)

Even in culture, leisure, and entertainment—let alone in finance and industry, America is now the laggard, not the leader.

These statements represent what I would call mainstream declinism of the technocratic center left, but in recent years there has also been a wave of center-right pragmatism. The two streams of thought converge on the idea that the US has, in fact, good underlying economic fundamentals despite the bad politics or stagnant culture. Two good examples of meliorist thinking are Hubbard and Kane's *Balance: The Economics of Great Powers from Ancient Rome to Modern America* (2013) and Acemoglu and Robinson's *Why Nations Fail* (2012). Both offer convincing statistical and econometric accounts of the US in relative decline. Both argue for institutional and political solutions (more inclusive than extractive, more bipartisan than gridlocked) to regenerate long-term growth and buoy up American power.

Mainstream declinism remains bedeviled by a fundamental question: When did—or will—decline happen? You can read a sampling of fifty, sixty, or seventy books published in the last twenty years and find no clear answer. Declinists generally want to alarm *and* reassure readers, leading to real confusion about the chronology of the US twilight. Is it eternal recurrence or sudden crisis? That defining contradiction—chronic decline and acute decline—obscures the less sensational truth: a fifty-year cycle of relative economic loss. Fifty years is too long to sustain a red-alert crisis mentality. But because it is omni-explanatory and always looming, the threat of Downsized America justifies policies based on scarcity and austerity. Stretching audiences between false alarm and false hope, declinism sells a fallacy: the idea that America can stay atop the global system indefinitely. But as the British ruling classes learned after 1900, there is no reversing history. Number one will always become number two someday. There is no permanent hegemony, only the illusion of permanence (Hutchins).

One reason the time line remains scrambled is that most declinist books are tracking the moving targets of policy outcomes and economic indices—contested facts and figures. They should also be tracking narratives and beliefs—culture, in a word. It's not that statistics and metrics are unimportant while fantasy and rhetoric are. It is rather that mainstream declinism is too invested in the explanatory power of the numbers. It is too invested in a model of political rationality, assuming that states and subjects respond on cue to economic facts. It is likewise too invested in a model of positivist history, assuming that we know what happened and why. When we center the discussion on voluntarist policy choices, known variables, and rational actor theory, we risk ignoring two significant and highly unruly factors: cultural myths and free-market speculation. These irrational and unknowable forces resist moral restraint, cognitive order, and the wonkish will of the policymaker. Belief trumps reason.[4]

Yet can-do technocrats of both center right and center left still dominate the decline debates. Hubbard and Kane, for example, think that Britain in 1900, with better economic tools and models, might have been able to "arrest the relative decline" (182). By extension, American policymakers, properly educated by economic data (which fails routinely to predict even local business cycles let alone macrohistorical changes), could arrest America's relative decline. Likewise Zakaria, who has a healthier sense of the limits of econometric thinking and an obvious appreciation for the forces of belief, nonetheless in the end argues that economic dysfunction in the contemporary US is largely due to "specific governmental policies" (233).

In recent years, the wonkish center has coalesced into a series of positions staked to the mitigation of American decline. Much valuable and subtle work abounds in these books, the technical analysis of which exceeds my brief. Meanwhile, though, the pragmatists have for the last twenty years been outshadowed by more fiery neoimperial thinkers like Niall Ferguson and Robert Kagan. For Ferguson and Kagan, the minibooms of the 1980s and 90s and victory in the Cold War cemented a powerful mythology of American might and right. The moral certainty of their viewpoints makes for compelling reading. They argue that American leadership is essentially benign and urgently needed. Both evoke the civilizing mission of the old British empire as a model. Kagan warns US policymakers against the ill-advised idea of "committing pre-emptive superpower suicide." His motto, credited to Charles Krauthammer: "Decline…is a choice." In his influential essay "Not Fade Away," Kagan argues that America has declined, but not by much, and that the "liberal international order" cannot survive without American power. Puzzling verb tenses back his claims: "American decline, if it is real, will mean a different world for everyone." Here is the essence of declinist language: a disaster will or might happen; either way, its consequences are assured in advance.

Ferguson, for his part, famously urged a righteous return to unapologetic US superpowerdom as a responsibility too often shirked by self-centered and soft-minded Americans who "would rather consume than conquer" (*Colossus* 29). He is the latest version of the British pundit urging leadership on decadent, dunderheaded, or isolationist America. We had the scholarly Paul Kennedy for the Reagan years, the iconoclastic Christopher Hitchens for the Clinton years, and the bluff neo-Victorian Ferguson for the Bush II years. Ferguson's books, *Empire* (2003) and *Colossus* (2005), provoked ferocious responses from the liberal left, particularly among professional historians of British imperialism and US politics. Along with David Cannadine's *Ornamentalism* (2002), Ferguson's books signaled a consolidated and media-savvy revisionism that rejected two decades of anti-colonial work in the university and decades of colonial resistance across the Global South. Imperial apologetics of this kind were vigorously disputed by Timothy Brennan, Antoinette Burton, Mike Davis, Catherine Hall, Pankaj Mishra, and Shashi Tharoor, among others. Harry Harootunian blasted the "resurrection of a phantasmagoric British Empire as a foundational historical experience and America's true imperial legacy" (103). Even now, Priyamvada Gopal and Priya Satia are pushing back against the redemptive vision of Anglo-American power that Ferguson helped repopularize: "In public memory, redemptive myths about colonial upliftment persistently mask the empire's abysmal history of looting and pillage, policy-driven famines, brutal crushing of rebellion, torture, concentration camps, aerial policing, and everyday racism and humiliation" (Satia 4).

Mainstream declinism uses the British precedent the wrong way. It focuses on the decline itself rather than its aftereffects. But the factors leading to UK and US loss of global economic advantage are baked into capitalism as a dynamic system. The response is what matters, not the inevitable (and relative) loss of hegemony. Moreover, to analyze underlying economic conditions is to miss the real payoff of comparative analysis between UK and US decline. The US is in a significantly better position in the 2020s than the UK was in the 1970s. But what *is* helpful and relevant is the cultural parallel. Here there are important similarities and here a difference can still be made.

Many Brexit commentators have noted that attachment to lost greatness remains a potent force for UK voters. No doubt that is true, and those residual attachments to empire have great monitory value for Americans as they reimagine their nation minus its eternal claim to be the richest, freest, strongest society on earth. Edoardo Campanella and Marta Dassù point out that restorationist claims are fueling state politics across the globe, from the UK and US to Russia, Turkey, Japan, China, and other nations with former imperial glory in their history (22–23). In surveying this phenomenon—a politics of nostalgic nationalism, they distinguish between "restorative nostalgia" (which anchors nationalist sentiment to "absolute truths") and "reflective nostalgia" (which puts such truths into question)(45). For Campanella and Dassù, Brexit marks a uniquely consequential and broadly democratic version of national nostalgia. But restorative nostalgia—the melancholy and defensive belief that supremacy is an American birthright—is gaining ground in the US as hegemony ebbs. Restorative nostalgia has emotional reach and bite. It encourages Americans to invest in past glory rather than work through a complex history.

Without a compelling and collective reconsideration of the national past, the US risks a long cultural tailspin (Brill). Reflecting on UK decline in 2004, Perry Anderson saw the tailspin that had absorbed his society's potential energy: "Britain's diminution since the war has been a long-drawn-out process…There was no dramatic reckoning with the past, just a gradual slide within a framework of complete political stability" ("Dégringolade" 3). Stagnancy was rooted in the failure of the historical imagination to overcome imperial nostalgia. The US stands now where Britain once stood, at the threshold of a dramatic reckoning. The signs are everywhere. The 2020s culture war is a history war, and it turns on the meaning of national decline and lost hegemony. American power depended on the arrogation of land, labor, resources, and wealth. Reckoning in the twenty-first century means, yes, mourning the loss *of* American greatness. But it also means mourning the losses that led *to* greatness.

As the new history wars unfold, the British precedent sheds light on several facets of American decline and division. For the UK in the nineteenth century and the US in the twentieth, a hegemonic mission—ruling the world in the name of freedom—produced a solidarity effect across classes at home. The expansive mission worked for decades to absorb nonelite and elite interests into what seemed like a unified mission. The breakup of that consensus culture has resulted in a deep sense of division and loss for many Americans. Fifty years ago, British society experienced a similar upsurge of regional, racial, and class tensions—precursors to the sharp red-blue, urban-rural, left-right, black-blue divides of the contemporary US. On the downslope, the fault lines of American society are cracking open (Kruse and Zelizer).

In a sense, the internal divides have become more salient now, and the afterlife of British power more instructive than the Roman and British analogies that proliferated in the early 2000s. Throughout the Bush II presidency, with its auguries of decadent neoimperialism, monitory books like Morris Berman's *Dark Ages America*

(2006), Paul Krugman's *The Great Unraveling* (2003), Michael Mann's *Incoherent Empire* (2003), Chalmers Johnson's *Sorrows of Empire* (2004), and Cullen Murphy's *Are We Rome?* (2007) shaped the conversation. Johnson offered a fiery, hard look at US militarism and its bad consequences: "Roman imperial sorrows mounted up over hundreds of years. Ours are likely to arrive with the speed of FedEx" (285). Murphy presented a more dispassionate view in the manner of the liberal journalistic observer. He usefully set out six parallels between late Rome and decadent America: solipsistic self-regard, discriminatory ignorance of the rest of the world, high militarization on a dwindling demographic base, corruption of the commonwealth by private interests, border troubles and immigration disputes, and sprawling managerial complexity (17–20). The Iraq and Afghanistan wars marked the drift of American power from hegemony to dominance, making the late Roman parallels almost irresistible. Just as tempting was the historical precedent of the Victorian New Imperialism, a hawkish turn to dominance that lasted to World War I. Of course, America was not a new empire after 9/11. It was an aging hegemon. Bernard Porter observed in his 2006 study that America was—in terms of lands and peoples conquered, in terms of military and economic advantage—fully as much an empire as Britain had been for centuries. It was, in fact, a "Superempire" (8).

The hot debates of the Bush years cooled into more academic reflections in the Obama years. The prescriptive brio of the moralists and the wonkish confidence of the technocrats now share space with a more philosophical tranche of declinist arguments. One vivid recent example is Ross Douthat's *The Decadent Society* (2020). Douthat gives a comprehensive account of an American society grown sterile and sclerotic. Tracking the latest signs of decay among Western elites, Douthat revives 1980s-style moral commentary, particularly with regard to the failures of religion and reproduction. But he also points to the baseline economic factors, synthesizing the work of Tyler Cowen and Robert Gordon into five key drags on American capitalism: aging demographics, massive debt, educational failure, technological inertia, and environmental limits.

The growing salience of environmental limits has forced a planetary view of US decline. For this reason the Big History type of declinism keeps getting bigger—more geological in depth, more cosmic in scale. Multi-century studies of demography, climate, epidemiology, migration, and technological innovation help readers to find an almost comforting Olympian viewpoint on the fate of civilizations. The rise of popular macrohistory for US readers reflects, I think, the "becoming historical" of American culture itself. This is an important fact: American readers are looking back for answers more than ever (Graeber and Wengrow; Harari).

One leading example of the new Big History was Jared Diamond's 2005 *Collapse: How Societies Choose to Fail or Succeed*. The how-to title captures the pop-pragmatism of so much declinist work, but the drift of Diamond's book is toward long trend lines not quick fixes. A more somber variant on this method is Joseph Tainter's *The Collapse of Complex Societies.* Tainter's book appeared roughly in sync with Kennedy's *Rise and Fall of the Great Powers* in the 1980s. His ideas—profiled on a 2020 cover of the *New York Times Magazine*—are back in heavy rotation.

Long-wave approaches to American decline continue to proliferate as anxious Americans navigate the Trump era and its hangover effects. Peter Turchin's *Ages of Discord* (2016) offers an idiosyncratic "cliometric" approach to US history mapped against economic data. Turchin's model identifies and predicts peaks of social instability around 1970 and 2020—dates that neatly correspond to deep crises of British and American power. The idea of civilizational decay has stoked the MAGA imagination, pulling once-dry fields of academic debate into the vortex of right-wing populism. Steve Bannon, the "intellectual" architect of Trumpism, picked up on the brooding millennial potential of *The Fourth Turning: An American Prophecy* by William Straus and Neil Howe. The reissue of that book bears the florid tagline "What the Cycles of History Tell Us About America's Next Rendezvous with Destiny." Bannon managed to see in this paperback prophecy a kind of Big History that could galvanize the energies and anxieties of disaffected, web-literate white men on the right. All sides in the history wars now have their macronarratives. Bannon's idea is to pose a restorationist white nationalism against *The 1619 Project* and its reframing of Black history/US history. Bannon's racist bloviating recalls the insidious 1960s and 70s rhetoric of the UK's Enoch Powell. Powell used an education in the high classics just as Bannon uses the ersatz authority of pop-megahistory to provide an intellectual patina for white moral panic.

Readers, publishers, and reviewers have given a great deal of attention to long-range historical thinking about US decline. But they largely ignore the most systematic, robust, and relevant body of work about the fate of the hegemons. I'm speaking about the historical analysis of materialist and Marxist thinkers such as Immanuel Wallerstein, Eric Hobsbawm, David Harvey, Giovanni Arrighi, Beverly Silver, Radhika Desai, Richard Lachmann, Robert Brenner, and Ellen Meiksins Wood, among many others.[5] Despite Benjamin Kunkel's attempt to popularize them, figures like these have been relegated to academic circles. In 2021, professional investor and amateur historian Ray Dalio published a high-profile trade book on the rise and fall of the great powers. Dalio follows the research trajectories of Hobsbawm, Silver, and Lachmann (for example) but describes his findings as more or less his "own research." He cites and acknowledges both Niall Ferguson and Paul Kennedy but not Arrighi and Wallerstein.

The pattern is quite clear. British pundits in the arena of Big History declinism and retro-imperialism appeal to an underlying American nostalgia for the moral and political confidence of hegemon culture. Educated US elites—not just MAGA adherents, but a broad swath of readers—keep borrowing from UK historians a center-right view of the imperial past. They tend to ignore the work of critical historians of empire such as Antionette Burton, Priyamvada Gopal, Pankaj Mishra, and Priya Satia. To bring these latter voices into wider public recognition would balance out the wishful (technocratic) and wistful (moralist) dimensions of popular declinism.

Detailed and deeply researched Big Histories of the kind provided in Arrighi's *The Long Twentieth Century*, for example, would also bring more clarity and more data to the conversation about US decline. Arrighi's methodology operates outside the alarmist/optimist binary of mainstream declinism. His book outlines a global pattern documented over long cycles of capitalist accumulation from the sixteenth century to the present. Each cycle is dominated by a great power—Genoese, Dutch, British, and American, in sequence. Each hegemon passes through both a signal crisis and a terminal crisis, with the fading power of their productive, commercial, and commodity-centered economies indexed by the rise of high finance and political violence. The British economy was, for example, increasingly militarized and financialized from the late Victorian period forward. Their signal crisis of the 1870s was prelude to the terminal crisis of the 1920s and 1930s, after which point the US became the center of the global economy (251). Following in that rough pattern one hundred years later, America after the 1970s began to lose its competitive advantage. Arrighi suggests that

American hegemony entered its "signal crisis" around 1975 and its "terminal crisis" after the Bush II wars (215). Over time, the US became an increasingly hollow hegemon, sustained by the false booms of tech, debt, and finance, all juiced by massive defense spending ("military Keynesianism").

From the viewpoint of short-cycle economists—more cockeyed optimists than dismal scientists!—the 1980s and the 1990s looked like the return of victory culture to the US (Gross). But the Reagan and Clinton recoveries were short-lived episodes within the longer history of what Robert Brenner has called the "long downturn." Brenner's account of post–World War II American capitalism corroborates the Arrighi model. The bursts of growth after 1975 that Arrighi calls miniature *belles époques* correspond to Brenner's concept of new, transient Gilded Ages. Times were good in the 1980s and 1990s for some Americans, some of the time. An echo of the old national greatness licensed new fantasies of sustained wealth. But the sanguine vision of self-perpetuating US economic power was built over an unsustainable base that featured growing—and socially destabilizing—debt and inequality (Brenner, "What's Good," 23). Sporadic bursts of market recovery do not fundamentally change the trajectory of deindustrialization and shrinking real wages for the middle 50% of Americans.

Brenner has provided a thick and technical description of what Arrighi calls the "Autumn of the System." His account turns on the observation that the US failed in the 1970s to "switch to new unfamiliar lines" of production in response to a growth crisis predicated on industrial over-capacity ("What's Good," 9).[6] Fareed Zakaria rightly notes the British were making too many bicycles and not enough cars in 1907. But few Americans understood in 1977 that they were making too many cars and televisions, not enough computers and solar cells. Massive state investment in old lines of production probably saved the economy from even more painful dislocations in the 1970s and 1980s. But it perpetuated a period of slow and artificial growth with no broad expansion of American prosperity. In the thirty-year period 1945–1975, household incomes doubled. Since then, they have essentially flatlined (Madrick). The financialization that has accounted for much of US growth since the 1980s does not need to be viewed in moral terms as a parasitic displacement of the "real" (manufacturing) economy. But it is a predictable index of relative economic decline, a massively anti-democratic shift of resources, and a "prelude to the terminal crisis" (Arrighi 371).

The facts remain: the US was the top manufacturing country for one hundred years leading up to 2010, when China took over (McCoy 23). Before that, Britain was the top manufacturing country for roughly one hundred years. These were the two interlocking ages of Anglo-American hegemony. Within that long arc of history, most economists consider 1950 to be an artificial peak for the

US. Immediately after World War II, the US generated 50% of global gross product. That number moved quickly from 50% to 40% during the 1950s, as Asia and Europe rebuilt. The peak era was in that sense already a downslope era. The US share of GGP (global gross product) settled in at 25% around 1980 and remained there for three decades. By 2010, at the start of the Obama years, the US was closer to 20 than 25% of GGP. And by 2020, that number had slipped to 16%. So the confident 1990s revivalists who believed that the US could go on holding a quarter of GGP (with an aging industrial, demographic, and infrastructural base) have been proven wrong in real time.

Consider these underlying numbers in a different way. George Kennan in his famous 1948 overview of postwar foreign policy noted that America had "50% of the world's wealth but only 6.3% of its population." His one key priority was to "maintain this position of disparity without positive detriment to our national security" in the face of "envy and resentment" (qtd in Desai 63). Leaving aside the strategic and ethical wisdom of perpetuating that gross wealth disparity, Kennan's numbers give us a baseline index for (crudely) measuring relative economic power. The Kennan Ratio, let's call it, holds that the proportion of global wealth to global population was roughly 8x for America in 1950. At its comparable peak in 1870, the British Empire had roughly 25–30% of global wealth and the UK had roughly 2–3% of global population. Their Kennan Ratio was something like 9x.

TABLE
*Kennan Ratios*

|  | National product as percent of global product | National population as percent of global population | "Kennan Ratio" |
|---|---|---|---|
| Britain at peak (1870) | 25–30 | 2–3 | 9x |
| Britain in 2020 | 2.5 | .8 | 3x |
| US at peak (1950) | 50 | 6.3 | 8x |
| US in 2020 | 16 | 4 | 4x |
| China in 2020 | 18 | 18 | 1x |

Today the Anglosphere's share of raw economic power is diminished and diminishing. Britain has about 2.5% of global gross product and 0.8% of global population. Its Kennan Ratio has contracted from 9x to 3x over 150 years. For most of the downslope decades since Kennan, the US has been at about 6x, with 25% of gloss global product and 4% of population. But the US is currently approaching 4x, as GGP hovers at 16% while population remains at about 4%.[7] Since 1950, America's economic advantage has been cut in half. For comparison's sake, China in 2020 had 18% of GGP and 18% of the global population for an even Kennan Ratio of 1x. When China does become the world's number-one economy, it will command only its own share of resources and wealth. That will break a five-hundred-year-old pattern not only of Western preeminence, but of intense and asymmetrical capital concentration under the flag of the greatest power. It seems unlikely that any future hegemon will attain the kind of disproportionate GGP share produced by British and American industry from 1810 to 2010.[8]

China, in other words, may never be a hegemon in a strict or familiar sense. And that is not just an economic fact. The last two hundred years of modernization have set cultural and political patterns that will continue to yield advantages to the US—most obviously English itself, the de facto global language of trade and technology. Arrighi's "terminal crisis" and Zakaria's "post-American world" probably evoke too stark a picture. Becoming the number-two economy does not mean the end of American hope, security, or prosperity. It does not, certainly, mean the end of American military dominance and strategic preeminence. Nor will living on the imperial downslope prevent the US from becoming a more perfect union or a more just society—quite the opposite, I would think.

But the next one hundred years will be different from the last hundred. By some accounts, the US will cede the title of largest economy to China as early as 2022. By the end of the 2020s, according to Standard Chartered Bank, "six of the 10 largest economies could be in Asia" (Martin). Some experts predict that the US will be number three to China and India before the midpoint of our century. In the last few years, US debt crested up over 100% of GDP. Meanwhile, China in 2020 became the top receiver of direct foreign investment—another measure of its economic eclipse of America. For those eager to believe in the eternal economic and political supremacy of the US, the signs littering the economic news will be harder and harder to ignore, even as Chinese growth slows. Decline is becoming a reality. But it is not the reality that most declinists brandish to scare (up) readers.

Although declinism is predicated on stories of national collapse and lost wealth, decline generally brings a very slow adjustment of national and global hierarchies. At a macro scale, the Dutch and British precedents confirm this point. Wealth exited those national systems only gradually after their respective peaks in 1700 and 1870 (Lachmann 434–436). The wealth of the British elites has lasted a great deal longer than their formal empire, as has the globally advantaged lifestyle of ordinary UK citizens. Even as the Chinese economy grows to outweigh the American one in raw size, Chinese GDP per capita will remain significantly lower than US GDP per capita. That statistic measures how people actually live and earn. At present, Americans are on average five times wealthier than Chinese citizens (Hubbard and Kane 44). The problem, of course, is the poor distribution of that wealth. When the US was a true hegemon, expansion (of wages and property) happened in the middle. Since the 1970s, almost all the increased wealth of America has been generated for the top 5% of Americans. In the face of such asymmetry, it is not hard to see why so many Americans believe—against logic—in the alarmist narrative of national collapse *and* in the reassuring narrative of long-term national superiority. Here again, ideological fantasies about American wealth have come to matter more than facts, figures, or the rational self-interest of nonelite voters.

The Sinophobic dimensions of declinism have been and will be shaping factors in Americans' ability to countenance the gradual-but-actual loss of economic supremacy. The other side of that Sinophobia is a set of fantasies that moralize Western/white superiority and view Asian accumulation as a civilizational—not just an economic—threat. The civilizational markers of Chineseness (Confucian or Communist) only partially mask the racial phobia underlying so much of the public rhetoric about China's eclipse of America. To be certain, there was plenty of Americaphobia in the UK from the 1890s through the mid-twentieth century. It channeled the same fears of lost greatness and national eclipse. But there was also an overriding narrative of succession from one liberal Anglophone superpower to another. The Anglo-Saxon "special relationship" smoothed over a fairly drastic shift in the global balance of power.

As power shifts from America to Asia now, such baton-pass fantasies of continuity do not cushion the blow of lost greatness. True, there is a necessary cooperative interdependence between Chinese and American capitalisms. But there probably will not be a culturally organized partnership such as the one forged between the UK and the US at Bretton Woods. The situation is still unprecedented in cultural terms. America was Britain's fraternal successor; China is America's strategic rival. A phobic cultural narrative hangs over the future of global power, crystallized in the notion of a "post-Western" world.[9]

The cultural fantasies attached to Western success and Western succession (UK to US) produced a literary trove of national virtue tropes. Traditional histories of the Great Powers recirculate those tropes: the Anglo-Saxon gift for freedom, the English flair for liberal governance, the American knack for technological breakthroughs, Anglo-American concepts of fair play, a natural love of free markets in the English-speaking world. The point here is not that these ideas are ethno-national nonsense, though they generally are. The point is that strategic power and economic success create cultural narratives that attach to moralized concepts of national or racial character. Apex powers believe in free peoples and free markets when they dominate the playing fields they call level. That is equally true of elite social fractions: they tend to believe in a narrative of superior character, skill, or effort as an account of their class power. These narratives are themselves powerful and tenacious. They have to be understood for their independent historical weight. Even if history makes those narratives and tropes of Anglo virtue ultimately obsolete, they will have outlived the economic formations that once supported them. It is for that reason, too, that cultural histories of declinism have to be advanced alongside, and sometimes against, the usual, supposedly objective or quantitative accounts of national decline.

US decline forces a reckoning between East and West and between Global North and Global South. It also forces a reckoning between the old North Atlantic powers and their long histories of settler colonialism, Islamophobia, resource extraction, and the racialized divisions of labor at world scale. Fading US hegemony challenges all Americans, but especially the elites who see national loss, correctly, as a projected loss of their own social advantage. Decline can and should be democratizing. For this reason, decline has triggered white/elite panic. Declinism too often has served as a sanitized proxy language for aggrieved groups (white, WASP, American—the interchangeability is the very point) who funnel their sense of loss into the language of national twilight. How can that narrative of a great nation betrayed be interrupted, challenged, or reversed?

Since this is a book about cultural history, the answer lies in how Americans absorb and transmit the story of American power, past and present. In the last five years, US and UK publics have become more and more attuned to the interlocking historical debates over racial equity and national greatness. Recent studies of imperial history by Adom Getachew, Jeanne Morefield, and Priya Satia have offered timely cases for a fuller reckoning with the racist legacies of empire. These are not new debates, but they are moving out of academic circles and into national conversations. Getachew, Morefield, and Satia, among many others, have begun to bring the entwined legacies of the English-speaking world together in a history of UK-US power that is also a global history of civil rights, racial capitalism, and anti-colonial struggle.

Similarly, James Baldwin famously saw that anti-Blackness in America could not be separated from the global project of Western imperialism. More American

voters see the force of Baldwin's insight now than ever
before. Pankaj Mishra summarizes the point:

> James Baldwin outlined the necessity of…a moral and intel-
> lectual revolution in the starkest terms, arguing that "in
> order to survive as a human, moving, moral weight in the
> world, America and all the Western nations will be forced to
> re-examine themselves," to "discard nearly all the assump-
> tions" used to "justify" their "crimes." The fire Baldwin
> imagined in 1962 is now raging across the US, and is being
> met with frantic appeals to white survivalism. . . . Under-
> standably, people exalted for so long by the luck of birth,
> class and nation will find it difficult, even impossible, to dis-
> card their assumptions about themselves and the world. But
> success in this harsh self-education is imperative if the prime
> movers of modern civilisation are to prevent themselves from
> sliding helplessly into the abyss of history. ("Flailing States")

To avoid the abyss of history, Mishra contends, US elites
must embark on a new kind of self-education. But as in
the UK, so in the US: citizens are split between reclaim-
ing national greatness and calling it into question. Paul
Gilroy observed ten years ago in his acute diagnosis of UK
postimperial melancholy "half the country's yearning to
be a different kind of place" (xii). Gilroy staked his book's
cautious optimism to the possibility that the UK could,
collectively and institutionally, make "its buried and dis-
avowed colonial history…useful at last as a guide to the
evasive, multicultural future" (xii). Americans interested
in a better future might take up the terms of Gilroy's hope
for themselves, accepting the risks and rewards of a new

kind of self-education without the "lure of greatness" (Barnett).

Learning to live as an ex-superpower and as a multira-cial democracy were major challenges for Britain in the post–World War II era. Back in the 1980s, Stuart Hall described what British culture had to overcome in order to shed the vestiges of national supremacy:

> We are up against the wall of a rampant and virulent gut patriotism. Once unleashed, it is an apparently unstoppable, populist mobilizer—in part, because it feeds off the disap-pointed hopes of the present and the deep and unrequited traces of the past, imperial splendour penetrated into the bone and marrow of the national culture….An imperial metropolis cannot pretend its history has not occurred. Those traces, though buried and repressed, infect and stain many strands of thinking and action, often from well below the threshold of conscious awareness. (*Hard Road to Renewal* 73)

Unconscious and visceral patriotism feeds on the myth of national greatness. In both the UK and the US, it cannot be banished easily. But it is for all that not graven in stone. In fact it was Hall himself—among others—who helped to show how jingoism was actively cultivated in Britain 1880–1920. A concerted campaign recruited "the people" into a popular base of support for imperialism— to put the "great" in Great Britain. It was done for a pur-pose, Hall argued, and it could be undone.

The same logic applies here and forms the basis for a galvanizing approach to US cultural history in the next decade or two. Giving up the ghosts of lost greatness here will be a major challenge. US power and growth in the post–World War II era set high expectations, and those expectations remain deeply embedded in American "gut patriotism." US supremacy was a rallying point in Cold War America and it still is. The habits of thinking like a number-one nation are visceral for both privileged and struggling Americans. But those habits can be challenged. Culture, not policy, is the field of contest for that challenge.

Cold War US culture sponsored the mythologies of the American farmer and worker, the miner and rancher, the steel man and the auto man—all of which made it irresistible for policy elites in the 1970s to retrench around old industries rather than develop new lines of production. Declinism, defined this way, means a cultural attachment to obsolete modes of production. Success welded one mode of industrial production to the bedrock of American identity—and it has not yet been dislodged. Even as the elites presided over a deregulated and financialized economy that flatlined the economic prospects of the middle class, ordinary citizens held to a vision of greatness staked to older sources of wealth and security. Workers were both the holy symbols and the immediate victims of American nostalgia for industrial dominance.

Cold War expectations—of industrial power, military dominance, national greatness, small government, free markets, high growth—have outlived their economic base. They are blocking the next stage of American progress. As long as American superiority remains a sacred tenet of official discourse even of the center left, it will foster supremacist thinking about Asian economic power, about African-American property, about Indigenous land reclamation, about Islamic religious freedom. To dislodge that supremacism means sweeping out the stale tenets, melancholic attachments, and visible contradictions of declinist thinking.

Unlike the UK, the US is still a young country built— at least theoretically—on a concept of open citizenship rather than settlement, on dynamic progress rather than fixed traditionalism. The US has many material and ideological advantages over the UK when it comes to fighting free of superpower nostalgia. Even when it becomes the second-largest economy, the US will still be the third most populous and the fourth-largest country in the world. And we have the instructive lessons of history before our eyes. We can see where the UK has succeeded in reimagining its national identity after greatness, and where it has so far failed.

The point of this book is not to wish away American decline, but to insist that life after hegemony need not be gloomy or disastrous. It may take fifty years for American parties, institutions, and public rhetoric to adjust to the pastness of "solo superpower" status. It will take much longer for the accumulated wealth of the American Century to be lost. But the culture of decline can be reshaped from within the arts, media, and humanities. The statues of Cecil Rhodes and Robert E. Lee are already falling.

Looking at the recent historical debates over slavery and reparation in the UK, Maya Jasanoff sees: "A myth countered, a history deepened, and a gesture of recompense. There may never be an end to reckoning, but such beginnings might help historians imagine broader forms of recovery and repair. That, too, could be a kind of progress" (84). What will it look like when postimperial cultures on both sides of the Atlantic are no longer, as Priya Satia puts it, "hostage to myth"(5)? For one thing, it will take a new way of thinking past both the sanguine and the scaremongering poles of the core declinist contradiction.

I have summarized the partisan ebb and polemical flow of declinism over the last few decades. The most remarkable fact about American declinism since the 1970s is its failure to change. In many ways, its basic intellectual contours have been frozen for decades. It is as if our models and our language are bound somehow to replicate the fundamentally conservative impulse to circle the drain down which our national vigor is said to be slipping. The American future is still haunted by the ghosts of greatness. They haunt the public mind, held in place by morbid attachments to superpowerdom. The systematic dismantling of declinist thinking is now an urgent project for cultural historians and US citizens alike. As a first step, the next chapter proposes ten theses designed to point past the current limits of declinism.

## 2 AFTER SUPREMACY: TEN THESES

*Thesis 1: American decline is neither catastrophic nor avoidable.*

There is no fork in the road ahead where Americans will choose between declining power or global preeminence. They have had both for decades. They have both now. Decline *and* preeminence have shaped American life for fifty years. Eventually and unignorably, though, preeminence will turn into eminence. The downslope from "sole superpower" is guaranteed by capitalist laws of motion that do not respect the idea of evergreen national supremacy. But relative economic decline is not a cliff dive for security or prosperity. Even one hundred years after its peak, the UK remains the sixth-largest economy in the world despite ranking twenty-first in population and seventy-eighth in territory. The US now ranks third in population and fourth in territory and with some favorable winds in terms of demographic and technological advantage. Barring climate collapse, the American economy will remain strong generations from now.

The British case shows us that slow, inevitable decline is not disastrous for an aging superpower—a case thoroughly made by George Bernstein's *The Myth of Decline*. In 1950s England, associated in the American mind with Orwellian bleakness and narrowed estates, the average citizen of the UK was probably faring better than before in terms of wages, food, housing, transportation, technology, and health care. The era of imperial contraction was for the UK, and could be for the US, an era of communal rebuilding and infrastructural renewal.

Yet mainstream American declinism cannot seem to settle between the poles of blithe optimism and grave alarm. Its core contradictions might be chalked up to a simple diversity of opinion—a healthy debate among experts of different stripes. But that misses the essential truth. Declinism taken as a whole produces for its elite readership a paralyzing conundrum. It splits the policy mind and the general public between disaster response and do-nothingism. Even after fifty years, it still distracts readers from the slow American eclipse because neither media discourse—liberal or conservative—*nor* the national ego wants to relinquish the top nation slot. American leaders still do not have a guiding narrative to help citizens come to grips with America's slow descent into the ranks of the leading nations. But the Great De-exceptionalization is already starting to happen.

*Thesis 2: The fate of American capitalism is not
the fate of global capitalism.*

Capitalism moved on and reorganized itself after British
power; it probably will after American power. Fredric
Jameson coined a useful formula for the age of climate
disaster: "It is easier to imagine the end of the world than
to imagine the end of capitalism" (76). It is likewise easier
to imagine the end of US dominance than the end of capitalism. Still, some observers believe that capitalism has
already hit its environmental limits or that an "age of secular stagnation" has set in (Summers). It remains an open
question as to whether the next stage of capitalism will
sustain genuine expansions of wealth and productivity.
Giovanni Arrighi's evocative concept of the "Autumn of
the System" describes the end of the US-led cycle of accumulation. Such an end spells many potential crises for
capitalism at large as global trade, credit markets, and cur-
rency arrangements enter a period of uncertainty. Still, a
multipolar world or an Asian-group hegemon might re-
anchor the capitalist system and initiate a new cycle of
accumulation. There is room for growth if the energy transition decommissions fossil fuel. After all, capitalization is
still radically uneven and largely incomplete. Much of the
Global South has not yet been industrialized nor absorbed
into the mass consumer habits of the Global North.

The fortunes of the American nation-state and of capitalism generally are now less entwined than they once
were. America's paramount role in the global economy

from 1945 to 1975 was a historical exception enshrined as a cultural norm. But the exception and the norm are both fraying in the 2020s. Before we can analyze the culture of decline (1975 to the present), before we can glimpse the culture that comes *after* decline (2030 and beyond), we have to peel apart the essential American condition from both local factors and larger contexts. Local factors include the vagaries of the business cycle. US equity markets have gone up and down in bursts along the trend line of relative economic decline since 1970. Panning back a bit, most economists rely on the hundred-year run of expanding value in US stocks as if it were a permanent ground condition, outside history. Few pan back far enough to consider the limit points set by climate change and by the relocation of capitalist energy to Asia.

Americans have long wanted to believe that *their* nation's decline is reversible. It is possible, of course, that major breakthroughs in biotech or clean energy will drive productivity, profitability, and real wages back up again, launching a reexpansion of American capitalism. Such an event would break the logjam of secular stagnation. But so too would a serious adjustment in aggregate demand at either the national or global level. As Radhika Desai notes, industrial overcapacity is only half the problem. The other half is the chronic weakness of "aggregate demand" (152). Desai refers to the problem of low wealth, low wages, and high debt among nonelite classes in the US and nonelite countries in the Global South. These are two potential engines of aggregate demand that have not been fully incorporated into the global economy. The potential shift to neo-Keynesian economics under Biden might recharge the US economy. To expand the purchasing power of tens of millions in the Global South—through debt forgiveness and higher wages—would likely recharge the global economy. Either way, the fate of capitalism itself in the next fifty years will depend less and less directly on the absolute health of US markets.

*Thesis 3: Global success leads to cultural and political stagnancy for apex nations.*

Superpowers eventually fail in the continuous modernization of their social, economic, and political systems. Corollary: *Ex*-superpowers bear a similar risk. For both Britain in the nineteenth century and America in the twentieth, the experience of peak power brought official state policy and unofficial national culture together around the mission of freezing history. It's no surprise that hegemons seek to hold their advantage and extend their stay at the top of the world system. That fundamentally conservative impulse also ends up impeding the progress of democracy and domestic politics. It outlives imperial power in the form of superpower nostalgia. And it explains the rightward drift of UK and US politics in the era of decline—not to mention the rightward drift of Russian politics after the fall of the USSR. All three of the Yalta Powers of 1945 were once megastates—hence the *U* in their names flagging a tense union of disparate parts. All three have struggled with democratic rot and authoritarian populism on the downslope. To borrow a John Le Carré line: "All power corrupts. The loss of power corrupts even more" (317). Putin's Ukraine war of 2022 only reinforces the core meaning of the Trump-Brexit era: the downward mobility of nations—linked to the downward mobility of formerly privileged castes and classes—produces a high degree of political violence and volatility.

To understand political volatility on the downslope, we can draw on the work done in the UK by historians Tom Nairn and Perry Anderson. I think of them as "first responders" to the full crisis of British capitalism after empire. Their goal was to assess the stubbornly conservative framework of UK culture and politics despite the transformations of the postwar welfare state. Their findings—the so-called Nairn-Anderson theses—yielded a host of insights that return now with stinging intellectual force in the contemporary US. They argued that overseas empire gave the British ruling classes an extended lease on social power, one that outlasted empire. With some adjustments, we can transpose their model from the ruling classes of Victorian empire to the technocratic elites of Cold War America.

The problem that galvanized Nairn and Anderson fifty years ago is the problem besetting the US now: how to reconstruct a modern political culture instead of chasing after lost greatness. Disappointed in the failure of his society to pivot away from its traditional hierarchies, Anderson described the UK as "historically becalmed." His analysis—fifty years old and from the UK left—converges with the core ideas of Ross Douthat, arguing in 2020s America from the right. Both Anderson and Douthat observe the phantom-limb effects left behind by the loss of supremacy. Those effects block the future. They distract citizens of the UK and the US from making a new account of their nation.

Many Americans—not just MAGA adherents—have a visceral aversion to the end of US supremacy. They remain attached to the decisive national fantasy of endless growth and infinite dynamism. But no hegemon stands forever. As early as 1951, Reinhold Niebuhr could see what was coming:

> [T]he opulence of American life has served to perpetuate Jeffersonian illusions about human nature. For we have thus far sought to solve all our problems by the expansion of our economy. This expansion cannot go on forever and ultimately we must face some vexatious issues of social justice in terms which will not differ too greatly from those which the wisest nations of Europe have been forced to use. (29)

The moment of endless expansion has now departed. To judge by the vexatious issues of social justice now upon America in the 2020s, the moment for new wisdom has arrived. The future of decline—the future *after* decline—will give Americans the chance to think differently, to imagine the US not as a shrunken backwater, but a nation ready to move forward without dominating the globe.

*Thesis 4: Declinism projects scarcity and austerity,
but even on the downslope elite nations and elites
within nations retain wealth for generations.*

It is hard to dispute that the US economy, like the British
economy before it, underwent a process of deregulation
during the decades of its relative decline. One conse-
quence of that deregulation has been the rise of free-market fundamentalism, an idea that allowed US elites since
1980 to claim an increasingly disproportionate share of a
shrinking pie. Put another way: the anti-democratic force
of empire-building lasts from the apex phase to the
downslope phase. Wealth inequity is a recognizable facet
of decline in both the US and the UK. Less often remarked
is the overall economization of US political and intellectual life in the last forty years (Applebaum). Everyone now
seems to follow the markets and heed business leaders.
Economic thinking and the thinking of economists (not
the same thing) have gained enormous influence over state
policy and over the way that ordinary Americans think
about their lives, families, values, and identities. The so-
called dismal science has ascended as American confidence
has dwindled. Oddly, noneconomists see economists as
reliable prophets of both endless growth and sudden disaster. Inside the turbid currents of the news cycle, these
prophets reveal that the economy is somehow always in
peril, yet always rebounding. Americans are trained to
worry about the economy day and night but also to sink
their faith—and retirement savings—in the idea of a stock

market that always grows. The core contradictions of declinism track closely to the mystified and contradictory authority of economic experts.

The two dominant models for modern macroeconomics come from Keynes and Hayek. They were developed within the milieu of two European empires in decline, the British and the Austro-Hungarian. Surely that casts some light on the fit between American declinism and the particular—which is to say, limited—vantage point of economics. Technocratic and econometric ways of thinking command enormous authority over the present, yet seem very little invested in deep thinking about the past (the history of human thriving) or the future (the limits to capitalist growth). The economistic worldview traps its public in a confusing present tense. It is the root source of the mixed message that American prosperity is imminently threatened yet conceivably boundless. The ability of American elites to sell nonelites a vision of scarcity in the present yet abundance in the future is the nucleus of declinist thinking. It is the underlying predicate for financialization. It is the alibi for the ferocious upward distribution of wealth. To accept hard work and low accumulation, nonelites have to believe in the value of their sacrifices. They have to believe in the current-fragility-yet-future-stability of the US economy. Here we tap the cognitive dissonance at the root of declinism's irrational appeal—greatness *has to* come back. Rather than describe the real risks and potential gains of slow decline, American declinism (of which MAGA is a lurid variant) has offered to its adherents a truly addictive pill forever fusing anxiety to reassurance (Berlant).

Working-class and middle-class Americans naturally crave the national comeback story. The propertied elites, too, remain invested in the regrowth of American capitalism as the ultimate happy ending to present concerns. That last group, at least, can be reassured by history on one point. Wealth is not easily lost by privileged and propertied households. It is slow to redistribute itself even on the downslope. Especially on the downslope. The research of Raj Chetty, Thomas Piketty, and many others has revealed just how limited upward mobility— the essence of the American Dream—has been in the last fifty years. Their research cuts against the doctrines of free-market fundamentalism that have ruled the political landscape since Reagan.

*Thesis 5: Hegemony describes an intranational and an international set of relations.*

Fading US power throws the future status of American elites into question even when it leaves their wealth intact. In both the British and American cases, the first decades of decline featured a retrenchment of elite power (inside the state) and imperial power (across the world) under what we might call the decline-dominance binary.[1] Dominant powers dominate without invoking the general human interest as their moral platform, whereas true hegemons insist that their power serves the general cause of humanity. Dominance is the sign of decline. In that sense, Trump marked the decisive shift to dominance when he isolated American power as purely self-interested. It marked the end of the consent-hegemony model in which US elites defined and arrogated to themselves the "best interests" of other nations. They gained the consent of subordinate classes and nations under the doctrine of liberal imperialism. Militarized force was more often implied than demonstrated, though US state violence—like Victorian British state violence during the Pax Britannica (Hensley)—defined the Cold War.

As the current crisis of US power evolves into its next stage, the future of decline is reopening. The latest contractions of national power are destabilizing the hierarchies formed and protected within the US. That's the linking mechanism at the heart of hegemony theory as it was crystallized by the Italian social theorist Antonio Gramsci. In effect there is a mechanical transfer of energy between national power and elite control. At the peak, they reinforce each other. On the downslope, they destabilize each other.

The expanding wealth of the middle class was both the cause and the result of US hegemony in the mid-twentieth century. The contracting wealth of the middle class is the leading economic indicator of lost hegemony now. Optimistic declinists, who argue that we can still use wise policy to extend US hegemony into the coming decades, tend to emphasize aggregate wealth and military dominance. But it is not a question of whether the US can eke out ten or even thirty more years of massive debt, militarized spending, and oligarchic rule. It is a question of whether an expanded cultural, political, and economic franchise can bring the bottom 90% of US society to a better life.

Viewed this way, the slow fade of US hegemony might mean an ongoing cleavage of nonelite citizens from the elite calling of national supremacy. The Trump era (which has not yet elapsed as of 2022) evolved in part through that cleavage: populisms of the left and right opposed so-called globalism. In the UK, the loss of the imperial mission has produced more right populism than left populism. Authoritarian drift inspired British intellectuals on the left to band together during the 1960s and 1970s in order to comprehend and combat it. In chapter 3, I take stock of their insights as a potential guide to US culture in the years ahead. The central point is simple. Superpower nostalgia afflicted Britain in the 1970s as it afflicts the US in the 2020s. As long as it does, it freezes the old social hierarchies, feeds toxic historical prejudices, and cements the authority of discredited economic theories that belong to the hegemonic past.

*Thesis 6: Belief in national superiority is part of the moral infrastructure of white supremacy.*

The claim that the US is the "greatest country in the world" is an article of political faith that few mainstream public speakers dare to disavow. It holds the center of public discourse. Until it relaxes its grip on the American imagination and on the language of civic belonging, it will be difficult to define or describe a more racially inclusive national future. And more difficult still to disentangle a popular, democratic vision of the US from a populist and racist one.

Cultural historians on the UK side have brought to the surface the hidden and coded connections between national superiority and white supremacy. Paul Gilroy's *There Ain't No Black in the Union Jack* captured back in the 1980s the tight correlation between a declinist viewpoint and white nativism.[2] During the most intense decline epoch of British cultural history—after the Suez crisis of the mid-1950s, a specific new form of racial crisis and white populism bedeviled UK society. It represented the most parochial and baleful aspect of a more complicated process that I described in an earlier study as "becoming minor." (Esty). It was also the subject of a landmark study, *Policing the Crisis*, in which Stuart Hall and his research team linked shrinking imperial horizons to "police-Black conflict." That same fateful conflict has rent the fabric of American cities with increasing visibility during this time of intensifying US decline.

*Policing the Crisis* names white moral panic *in an ex-superpower* as the predicate for the anti-Black fear and violence. What England meant, Hall and his team argued, was "forged in relation to the superiority of the English over all other nations on the face of the globe." They continue:

This is basically an imperial image—its myths and ideological power are rooted in the policies and populist justifications of the high noon of British imperialism; into it has fed centuries of colonisation, conquest, and global domination. It is present in the Englishman's divine right to conquer "barbaric" peoples, a right which is then redefined, not as an aggressive economic imperialism, but as a "civilising burden." The Empire, backed by military, naval, and economic supremacy, helped to form the belief that the English possessed special qualities as a people which protected them from military defeat, and kept the country independent and secure. (147)

This passage, crafted in the days of terminal UK decline, slices right through fifty years of time to land in the US present in what James Vernon calls an "uncanny echo of our own times."

As long as US citizens are trained to believe in a glorious history of manifest destiny and innocent dynamism, as long as they are trained to repeat the mantras of national greatness, the logic of superiority will afflict race relations. Rather than catastrophize the prospect of dwindling American hegemony as an elite crisis, US leaders might instead give voice to the aspiration of living in a decent, humane, and multiracial society. The US need not aspire to be the Greatest Nation on Earth. As the material bases for US exceptionalism fade and fray, Americans have the opportunity to bring into daylight the white supremacy lurking inside the language of national greatness.

*Thesis 7: Rise-and-fall rhetoric frames the
expansion of empire as a masculine adventure.*

Corollary: Declinist rhetoric frames the *contraction* of
empire as a tale of beset manhood and betrayed nation-
hood. No analysis of mainstream declinism's current
intellectual limits is complete without noting that rise-
and-fall tropes have been woven into a heroic and mascu-
linist concept of state power. They are also woven into
the tragic, often covertly masculine, narrative of *lost*
power. Gender's importance to the language of national
fate is unmistakable. Yet it is also subtle and indirect,
lodged below the conscious threshold of facts, data, and
models. It is therefore rarely addressed in the trade-book
annals of American declinism.

The epic casting of the Rise and Fall of the Great Powers tends to be a genre of historical writing dominated by
men and featuring a version of Great Man history. The
ascent of Trumpism and the defeat of Hillary Clinton in
2016 was fueled by a blaring language of masculine
*revanche* welded to white nationalism. The sense of
aggrievement that drives authoritarian populism is not
just a matter of the "forgotten white working class," but
of men who feel that modernization processes are passing
them by, diminishing their prospects, and stealing their
identity. The bald gender traditionalism of the MAGA
movement is obvious. But even for Americans who are
well left of Trump, a great deal of masculine nostalgia
attaches to the old, fading idea of America's ineffable

greatness. The sentimental link of lost manhood and lost greatness runs the political gamut, especially in times of national self-doubt. Aaron Sorkin's liberal paean to great men, cited in chapter 1, captures the wonkish strain of US machismo. Its roster of great men includes not just Eisenhower, Kennedy, and Glenn, but the engineers, researchers, and rocket scientists who made the US military-industrial complex into a world-beating dynamo.

Now male experts feel sidelined by the prospect of American twilight. Beset manhood, notes the critic Nina Baym, forms the core of many popular American genres. Declinism is one of those genres. No wonder, then, that women historians and feminist scholars have provided some of the strongest counterpoints to the rise-and-fall epic that dominates public discussions of destiny and decline. For students of the British Empire such as Antoinette Burton, Hazel Carby, Caroline Elkins, Catherine Hall, Anne McClintock, and Priya Satia, good history demands an awareness of gender and power at every level. Consider Elkins's account of the unconscious drive for masculine control in colonial Kenya (209) or McClintock's account of paternalist fantasies among administrators in British South Africa (232–257).

Such histories reveal the vital meeting points of gender and power in the old colonial fields of action. But classic imperial narratives also perpetuate a masculine ethos of heroic struggle even in newfangled *retellings* of that past. To produce what Burton calls "a more fugitive empire history" requires historians to address the tropes of lost greatness alike with gender in mind (220). Women historians have led a skeptical charge against imperialist apologetics and against the declinist fetish of lost greatness. Satia, for example, describes academic history's close relationship to imperial epic. She notes that the "inclusion of women and people of color" in the discipline has challenged traditional accounts, shifting in its turn the masculine texture and tragic ethos of grand history (2).

*Thesis 8: Epic tales of imperial rise-and-fall distort the narrative of national decline.*

The story of civilization as a rolling western epic is almost irresistible. It has grandeur and simplicity. It takes us in a regal swoop from Egypt to Greece, Greece to Rome, Rome to Christendom, Spanish Empire to Dutch, Dutch to British, British power to American hegemony. Surely part of this narrative's appeal comes from the satisfying application of tragic fate (those who rise must fall) and the projected logic of human mortality (all things must end). It also provides the metahistorical observer with a high vantage point. It blazes a single trail of explanation through the vast unknowns and entropic details of history. It Westernizes the Middle Eastern "cradles of civilization," and it ignores the economic power of Asia before the eighteenth century (Abu-Lughod, Bin Wong, Frank, Pomeranz). The traditional appeal of this story—sometimes called *translatio imperii*—has been that it begins and ends in the West.

The notion that America stood as the final culmination of civilizational striving is now itself in duress. The future of decline demands a new script.

Those who want to warn Americans about their fall often seem mesmerized by this familiar litany: *The Decline and Fall of Rome, The Rise and Fall of the Great Powers, The Collapse of Complex Societies, How Societies Fail, Weary Titan, Colossus.* These cadences ring out like bells. They shape the grand plot of decline even when their users try to work against their logic. There's a curious paradox by which many commentators who want to prescribe action and policy to fading America also want to evoke the enthralling and tragic story of the fall. How challenging it is to try to turn the grand movements of history against themselves, to save America from this iron logic of succession!

In the indelible classic motif of the crumbling Colossus or weary Titan, the long arc of prestige history meets the quick payoff of journalistic urgency. Rise-and-fall rhetoric provides the high-profile books with the feel of deep context carried in a light intellectual kit bag. Academics and popularizers alike use Britain and Rome (and all the other dead empires) to spotlight the spectacle of US decline. The spectacle itself is the problem. To combine the inevitabilities of tragic history with the language of the how-to manual is, in the end, oxymoronic.

The lure of the declinist headline is now as strong in America as it has been in the UK since World War II. Weary-Titan thinking evokes the tragic force of Shelley's famous lines: "I am Ozymandias, king of kings, / Look on my works, ye Mighty, and despair! / Nothing beside remains." But much does remain in the afterlife of a superpower. To live through and past the Autumn of the System requires a different vocabulary, a less epic set of narrative conventions. It requires collected and collective analysis of fading hegemony as a set of challenges and opportunities. It requires that we view the waning era of national supremacy as a time of activity, change, dynamism, and thriving, not melancholic backdrift.

*Thesis 9: The historical experience of the UK establishes the contours of decline culture, but American patterns will be different.*

The baleful effects of superpower nostalgia are not nearly as inevitable as the bare facts of national decline. During their peak epochs of global power, Britain and America both claimed the cause of human liberation as a universal project organized under their flag and stapled to their national character. The qualities so often championed in the name of British or American exceptionalism—special gifts of freedom, fairness, innocence, energy, effort, enterprise, invention, and self-government—track more to the raw language of power than to any kind of special ethno-national talent or gift. The innate superiority of the English-speaking peoples is an idea with an unfortunate past and a tenacious hold on the historical imagination. But its grip is loosening. Present conditions are undoing the foundations of Anglo exceptionalism and scrambling the Western logic of succession.

Within academic disciplines, British and American myths of freedom have been under serious scrutiny for decades. But now the scrutiny is more than academic—it is at the center of American public life and conversation. Having once arrogated to themselves the dream languages of enlightenment, liberation, and modernity, the twin Anglo powers are now seeing their national myths put to new tests in broad daylight, by a broad public. To retire Anglo-American exceptionalism is no easy task, especially in the face of ex-superpower melancholia. In place of the old exceptionalisms buoyed by power and influence, we now find brittle defenses of Western freedom, too exhausted to hide their mean racial predicates.

British imperial thinking once served as a foundation for US hegemony and has continued to shape American concepts of decline. Too often the imaginative value of British history for American audiences has lain in nostalgic evocations of crown, empire, and social hierarchy. But there are other ways for Americans to use British history. It provides immediate and relevant models for our own history wars, particularly when it comes to reckoning with slavery and colonialism. Instead of reading Niall Ferguson's *Colossus* in a mass-market Penguin paperback, American students and citizens might consult Catherine Hall's *Legacies of British Slave-Ownership* and its collaborative website (https://www.ucl.ac.uk/lbs/).

Post-1945 UK history offers many potential lessons about national life on the downslope. The future of decline in the US will be quite different from the present in the UK and for a host of reasons. But American historians tend to overstate the unique path that the US took to global superpowerdom. In fact, the architects of Cold War US foreign policy deliberately invoked the example of Victorian liberal imperialism. At Bretton Woods, American leaders aspired to emulate the success of British hegemony (Desai 15). Decades later, the US trod in the footsteps of UK financialization. As Adam Tooze notes in his superb synthetic account of the 2008 crash, UK liberalization of trade and banking "acted as a crowbar to dislodge regulation worldwide" (82). Laissez-faire ideas have been emanating from the land of Adam Smith and the financial temples of the City of London for centuries. And they have been influencing US economic and cultural narratives for just as long.

British decline foretells the American downturn, but British declin*ism* leaves open several paths for national renewal on this side of the Atlantic. Americans need not follow the track to Brexit-style isolation and retrenchment, nor the track to national breakup. The US has many advantages at present, beginning with scale. The US internalized the land of its settler-colonial past, leaving it with a continent-sized territory, population, and domestic market. Long-term economic indicators are much better for the US now relative to comparable points in UK history. The US is still attracting new capital investment and new immigrant populations. Even though—and perhaps because—planetary climate crisis sets hard limits on economic growth, the prospects for

American cultural and social renewal are good. It requires intellectual and political effort to shift the grounding concepts of national identity. But it has been done before. It was done to build wide support for the idea of UK and US supremacy. It can be done to build wide support for UK and US cultures reimagined *without* supremacy. That prospect—that *project*—brings us to the most important thesis of these ten.

*Thesis 10: Narratives about decline are more powerful than metrics and statistics.*

Mainstream declinism concentrates too much on facts and too little on fictions. Paradoxically, a study of the fictions—the beliefs and ideologies—that have been shaping American culture is more objective and more useful than a flat-footed debate about the "facts." Cultural narratives of national loss are more influential in the real world than contested statistical realities. They are also a more stable object of study over time. In mainstream declinism, the economists, the historians, and the political scientists offer competing accounts of decline's past, present, and future. Their arguments turn on incommensurate and imperfect data sets. Econometric thinking is surely good for a thousand vital tasks, but it distracts from our ability to analyze America's destiny in deep historical context. What matters most is not finding the ultimate quantitative benchmark or infograph, as if the data will finally tell us how far the US has been or will be eclipsed. What matters is when and whether Americans (and which Americans) believe that the eclipse is happening. The question of belief is a cultural one. Far from being a soft or secondary humanities question, it is the very nucleus of the matter. Any capitalist understands that in a speculative economy, future value depends on the beliefs and expectations that govern decision-making regardless of the (supposed) facts on the ground.

Cultural narratives, horizons of expectation, symbols of belonging—identities, affiliations, and mythologies of national greatness lost, found, or abandoned: all of these are, in the end, important facts on the ground. We can study them. We can put them in context. We can compare them, and we can assess their effects on US society. Yet few high-profile declinists take cultural history as seriously as policies and metrics. Cultural narratives have their own tempo, quite apart from the facts and figures said to underlie them. Perceptions leap ahead of or lag behind the statistics used to graph the fate of the nation. Japan is now on the downslope from an economic peak (by GDP share and growth rate), but David Pilling has observed that it remains a successful, high-functioning society with rising standards of living (12). When life was good for the ruling class in the Edwardian UK, there was a prevailing sense of hope. When life was getting better for a wide swath of the lower-middle class in the 1960s, there was a prevailing sense of loss. In the US, morbid symptoms of declinism flared up even during the Eisenhower era. It was a salient part of the paranoid Cold War that the most powerful superpower ever was held together by the Red Threat. That never made economic sense, but it still makes cultural sense.

There is always a mismatch between the facts of structural decline and the myths, symbols, and feelings that set a declinist mood. Mainstream declinism is invested in political rationality, assuming that states and citizens respond on cue to economic facts. It is invested in a positivist view of history, assuming that we know what happened and why. Because declinist rhetoric so often aims its reflex "how-to/can-do" at a slow, deep process of decline, it finds itself claiming a "facts over fantasies" position while advancing—however subtly—the underlying fantasy that American supremacy can be indefinitely extended. Mainstream declinism is thus *too* deterministic about the catastrophic results of a US eclipse, but not deterministic *enough* about the likelihood of that eclipse. To address the future of decline is to resolve that paradox. We cannot reverse structural decline, but we can act to change the meaning of US society in the post-peak era. There is no need for more desperate attempts to salvage an outmoded and elite worldview in which the only safe world is one in which America is number one forever. If Americans let go of the Cold-War-era view that their preeminence is the predicate for security and prosperity, they might consider in a cooler historical temper the real prospects for a diverse and dynamic society in the coming decades.

The next few decades will determine whether the US adapts—more quickly and more successfully than the UK did—to its loss of paramount status. The 2020s history wars ask citizens to reconsider the meaning of American power. British and American publics are learning all over again about the achievements celebrated in—*and* the damages charged to—their countries' names. That challenge puts the long history of slavery and settler colonialism at the center of public debate. It sets new research and teaching priorities for the humanities disciplines in US universities.

The struggle to redefine national culture after empire has been underway for generations in the UK. To gather insights from it, we can revisit an extraordinary body of work in cultural history produced in the 1960s and 1970s by the British New Left. I think of the UK historians of that time—especially Stuart Hall, Tom Nairn, Perry Anderson, Raphael Samuel, Eric Hobsbawm, E. P. Thompson, and Raymond Williams—as intellectual "first responders" to the contraction of British power. They developed a genuine *theory* of national decline. Their synthesis of politics and culture gives us the most integrated way of approaching both actual decline and superpower nostalgia (declin-*ism*) in the contemporary US.

The achievements of the British New Left were catalyzed by an urgent and collective sense of mission. They wanted to make sense of the UK's rightward political drift, to understand the aftereffects of Britain's industrial, imperial past, and to map out the conditions for a more democratic, equitable, and secure future. For those of us working now in US media and institutions, the same urgent mission has announced itself. Cultural analysis and the history wars matter in the civic and political life of the US, which is now facing its own "Autumn of the System" moment. Two key premises are embedded in this claim: (1) culture matters and (2) the cultural history of the UK in the 1970s pertains to the current state and future outlook of American decline. Let's examine each premise in turn.

## CULTURE MATTERS

Here is Stuart Hall on UK culture after empire:

> The culture of an old empire is an imperialist culture, but that is not all it is, and these are not necessarily the only ideas in which to invent a future for British people. Imperialism lives on—but it is not printed in an English gene. In

    the struggle for ideas…bad ideas can only be displaced by
    better, more appropriate ones. (*Hard Road* 73)

What was needed, Hall wrote, was for "modern thoughts"
to displace imperialist nostalgia. But to dismantle the old
jingoist appeal of British greatness, those modern
thoughts, those better ideas, would have to "grip the
popular imagination, bite into the real experience of the
people." Hall's principle motivates this book. The struggle over history matters, and good ideas can dispel morbid superpower nostalgia. Perhaps the most important
thing that the New Left has to say to Americans of the
2020s is that the politics of national greatness are not
natural or permanent. They required an organized effort
to produce and are therefore subject to change. "Ideological transformations," Hall wrote, "do not take place
by magic" (47).

Hall himself observed how successfully Britain sold its
imperial project to the working class and to the lower-
middle classes in the late Victorian period. Jingoist elites
using the new media of the time pulled popular desire
toward ruling-class concepts of British destiny. They
siphoned class antagonism into emotional, patriotic support for crown, empire, and army. The heroic languages
of imperial romance and adventure habituated elites and
nonelites alike to the glories of British greatness. The rise
of this brand of nationalism facilitated what Tom Nairn
calls the "political baptism" of the working class (31). It
worked across class and regional lines, even after the two
world wars and the imperial twilight. Many Brexit voters

have never stopped conjuring the lost ideal of a Greater Britain.

In the US, the political baptism of the nonelites to the hegemonic mission happened in the years between 1920 and 1960. Mass culture in those crucial years paved the way for a patriotic politics built around US military prowess, massive expansion of literacy and lifestyle, the phobias of the Red Scare and Jim Crow, and commercial success across the globe. By the midcentury, anticommunism produced a coordinated ideological effort at cohesion. Elites recruited the political aspirations of working-class and middle-class voters into the cause of American supremacy, framing the export of American consumer capitalism as the triple gift of sacred freedom, true democracy, and general prosperity. The Hollywood studio system picked up the plots of late-Victorian adventure genres, adapting them to the worldview of US supremacy and global centrality. Of course, many Americans never bought that version of national greatness. Many never felt included in the Cold War version of manifest destiny. But enough did. And many still believe in an exceptional greatness for America, over and above all other nations. A consequential majority, I think, have been trained to accept the orthodox vision of boundless growth and evergreen supremacy for America. But Hall's history reminds us that gut patriotisms, however deeply held, have been changed in the past. They can be changed in the future.

## DIAGONAL HISTORY: UK THEN, US NOW

I am advancing two arguments about Anglo-American decline, one more familiar than the other. They do not mutually exclude each other, and each is instructive. The familiar one is that the Anglo powers, and the West generally, have experienced similar kinds of industrial contraction, fraying social consent, and dilapidation of the postwar welfare state since the 1970s. From this point of view, history is moving in rough parallel across the Atlantic. The messy 1970s gave way to the tandem ascent of Reagan and Thatcher and the rise of the Washington Consensus. The Clinton-Blair, Bush-Cameron, and Trump-Johnson or Trump-Brexit epochs represent short parallel cycles plotted against the slower, deeper curve of Robert Brenner's long downturn. The declinist and dreary 1970s were experienced in direct tandem, and each gave rise to a significant intellectual formation called the "New Left" in both the UK and the US. Both movements militated against traditional social hierarchies and opposed the "New Right" thinking of figures like Enoch Powell and Margaret Thatcher in the UK, Barry Goldwater and Ronald Reagan in the US.

But from another point of view, the UK and US have experienced the loss of supremacy in offset tandem. They face comparable challenges in becoming ex-hegemons, but they face those challenges under sharply different circumstances, unfolding fifty to one hundred years apart. From this perspective, post–World War II UK politics and culture *anticipate* rather than coincide with contemporary US politics and culture. This hypothesis cuts against the familiar view by positioning Trump, not Reagan, as the American Thatcher. The Thatcher-Trump comparison is not a direct claim about personality or even policy. It's a claim about the social crises that produced a decisive rightward lurch in domestic politics. Like Thatcher, Trump marks a breakdown in national consensus and global confidence—one that preexisted and outlasted her administration. Trump's administration, like Thatcher's, reflected *and* exacerbated the class, race, regional, and ideological fault lines of its society. Trump governed by dominance and division with an embattled white minority as his base.

By contrast to both Thatcher and Trump, Reagan was a more hegemonic leader. His presidency gained support across a wide range of regions and classes. The rightward lurches of the Nixon and Reagan eras were not nearly as radicalized as the rightward lurch of Trumpism, a measure of the thinning, stretching, hopeless distance Trump voters feel from the glory days of American greatness. The usual account of Reagan's success among working-class voters in the US turns on pocketbook issues or values conflicts (guns and abortion, chiefly). The Reagan version of US conservatism succeeded in pulling working-class whites to the right, but it also exerted gravitational force on urban and liberal elites who then willingly supported Clinton-style policies on crime and welfare. If we pan back from domestic social issues to consider the broad history of superpower rise and fall, we can see that the rallying point of US national power was becoming *the* cause during the late twentieth century. The fantasy of restored greatness was the symbolic basis for Reagan's well-nigh Churchillian success at unifying voters. It was still plausible then, but—as we now see—the less plausible the phrase "make America great again," the more powerful its ideological force. Even when Thatcher won victory easily (1987) and rattled the old British sabers in the Falklands, few believed in British supremacy.

Viewing history along the diagonal, comparing the UK 1970s and the US 2020s as epochs of division and decline, is a bit crude, given all the differences to be factored in. But the common points and resonances justify an initial run of the experiment. Imperial retreat happened earlier, faster, and harder in the UK than it has or will in the US. And because the UK patterns are more vivid and sharply curved—because they operate within a smaller national frame and can be assessed in hindsight, they throw American decline culture into relief.

## THE IMPERIAL DEEP FREEZE

The US now stands at a switch point of history as the UK once did. Perry Anderson's overview of postwar UK society probably sounds familiar:

> Today Britain appears an archaic society, trapped in past successes, now for the first time aware of its lassitude, but as yet unable to overcome it. These symptoms of decline have

been catalogued too frequently to need much repetition here: stagnant industries, starved schools, run-down cities, demoralized rulers, parochial outlooks. All these sores of the present have their origins in advantages of the past. (*English* 43)

The UK became trapped in its own myths of greatness, its own mystified concepts of free trade and liberal hegemony, its own ossifying social institutions and traditionalist manners. The US has been sleepwalking into this British trap for the last forty years, circling back to mid-twentieth-century ideas that "made America great" rather than generating, piloting, testing, and adapting new ones.

Not everything that is wrong with the US at present can be explained by relative economic decline or the pall of superpower nostalgia. For example, authoritarian populism has mushroomed all over the world in the last ten years, from India to Eastern Europe to the US. But the British precedent illuminates certain aspects of right populism and white nationalism that are particular to the Anglo ex-superpowers. In the 1960s and 1970s, British New Left thinkers wanted to make sense of UK culture and society after empire. They decoded the icons of Britishness: crown, empire, the City, finance, fair play, class hierarchy, empiricism, laissez-faire and, of course, traditionalism itself. They rethought the motor forces of British life from the ground up, seeking to assay the often pernicious legacies of lost greatness. Baffled at the tenacity of old Victorian hierarchies in a mass democracy, they wondered whether a full modernization of British politics would ever take place.

One core platform of New Left thinking, the so-called Nairn-Anderson theses, held that Britain's ideological horizons were set by an early revolution, early industrialization, and a successful tradition of class compromise between the aristocracy and the middle class. Class compromise produced social stability but extended the influence of the ruling classes well past their time in history. Even in the urbanizing, industrial decades of the nineteenth century, aristocratic values fed, and were fed by, the growing role of overseas empire. In fact, the Victorian empire was a kind of historical deep freeze for UK class relations. Anderson again: the empire gave "its characteristic style to [British] society, consecrating and fossilizing to this day its interior space, its ideological horizons, its intimate sensibility" (24).

British dominance in the global economy (1820–1920) extended the life-lease of the ancien régime: "The late Victorian era and the high noon of imperialism welded aristocracy and bourgeoisie together into a single social bloc" (Anderson 29). But when UK military and economic power started to wane, so evidently did the bedrock logic of class compromise. What Martin Wiener calls the "decline of the English industrial spirit" drove a wedge between the aristocrats and the capitalists, especially in the decades from 1880 on. The general strike of 1926 marked a further class divide, this time between labor and management.

Yet the elite vision of British society—and many aspects of the old class system—have survived decades of decline and division in the twentieth century. Here was the real mystery—the one the New Left has been trying to unravel for decades. Decline exacerbated rather than mitigated the hierarchies of the Victorian age. It reinforced rather than loosened the conservative grip on the popular imagination. And here is where the New Left model—in both its blindness and its insight—becomes fascinating for readers in the contemporary US.

The New Left urgently wanted to find a unified field theory of UK political history. Why was there no transformative labor movement? Why was social antagonism splitting along lines of race, region, religion, and ideology rather than class? Why devolution (of Scotland, for example) and not revolution? What made Thatcherism tick? Nairn, Anderson, and their colleagues sought a historical explanation for the success of the right wing at speaking to the legitimate fears of middle- and working-class citizens in a stagnant economy.

When they moved beneath elections and institutions, into the cultural roots of modern political alignments, the answers began to gel. Their research pointed to deep matters of attitude, belief, and identity—many of them associated with old habits of national superiority and the conservative hangover of empire. For example, Nairn observed: "The continuity of England's incredible myth-consciousness, and her political decay, are the products of a material history—the shrinking material basis of an imperialist order still trapped in its own historical contradictions" (276). Britain's growth made England a rich but hollow center.[1]

The New Left line of analysis captures two paradoxes about superpower culture that are worth revisiting for their counterintuitive relevance to US politics now. First, the British Empire cultivated the idea of a *weak* state. Its mythology? That free markets, stable class relations, an ideology of "fair play," and massive naval superiority all reduced the need for state intervention (wars, invasions, draconian laws). Second, the British Empire produced a *weak* and flexible rather than a strong and rigid nationalism at its English core. Its mythology? That the British center—specifically England—constituted a technical, universal, and composite modernity rather than a delimited or narrow way of life. It was more a civilization than a culture—a neutral hub around which could be arrayed innumerable satellite cultures each with their own religions, languages, and distinctive traditions. National identity at the center became invested less and less in customs or values, more and more in the relatively bloodless pursuit of growth itself. Greatness defined that nationalism. It was about governing ideas, not robust traditions. Britain was in that sense a metaculture or multiculture in its imperial heyday, with power emanating from an unmarked and tacitly white, tacitly English core.

Once peeled apart from its empire, England became both core and remnant. New Left analysis linked the cultural aftermath of empire to the conservative capture of working-class political energy. They began to study the social effects and expressions of the diminishment felt by (white) UK citizens after empire. Lost greatness drove authoritarian populism in the run-up to Thatcher. Stuart

Hall captured this political math: "The anxieties of the many are orchestrated with the need for control of the few" (35). The phrase rings out with contemporary American resonances. When even economically secure citizens feel that "traditional loyalties to street, family, work, locality" are eroding, conservative elites can recruit nonelites by channeling a shared but often unnamable sense of loss.

In the early days of Thatcher's campaign to "Make Britain Great Again," Hall wrote: "Entities of power are dangerous when they are ascending and when they are declining and it is a moot point whether they are more dangerous in the second or the first moment" ("Local," 25). In *Policing the Crisis*, he and his cowriters addressed the sensational media coverage of UK muggings during the 1970s. They argued that the shrinking contours of Britain served as one crucial predicate for a moral panic around urban street crime. That in turn served as the predicate for a new wave of law and order thinking and, eventually, for Thatcherism. The media stoked the crisis by framing young Black men as a social threat, converting them into "Folk Devils" (161). These were some of the racial ABCs of right populism forty years ago, and they were linked by Hall and his team to the rise of paranoid thinking. Conspiracy theories teem and simmer in a country on the downslope. After decades of imperial expansion, ordinary UK voters learned to view dissent or dissonance within the UK as "a conspiracy against 'the British way of life'" (23). Where the targets are vague and sinister, and a sense of loss prevails, conspiracy thinking quickly becomes racism. No wonder Englishness was prone to curdle into nativism of the kind advanced by Enoch Powell. With the imperial mission of growth, greatness, and overseas rule evaporating, national sentiment in England had nowhere to go.

## THE COSTS OF SUPERPOWER NOSTALGIA

The American story picks up from the English one here. As we move on the diagonal, across the Atlantic, from 1970 to 2020, the trails marked by the New Left historians lead to a more synthetic understanding of the complex life of an aging superpower on the downslope. The cardinal features of decline culture identified by the New Left have all become unignorable aspects of US culture and politics: repetitive cultural scripts and stale thinking in media, academic, and political institutions; a deregulated and heavily financialized economy; ossified class relations featuring a holdover alliance that keeps non-elites voting against their economic self-interest; melancholic attachments to lost power that result in a morbidly conservative politics; popular and populist anxiety about the national future; contagious political myths predicated on the imaginary betrayal of the nation's true essence; authoritarianism; white nationalism; white moral panic; the rise of control society and the carceral state; and widespread paranoia and conspiracy-theory thinking.

All of these problems plague the contemporary US as the downslope steepens. Taken together, they point to the cultural malaise and political vacuum produced by economic decline. Declinist ideas fill that vacuum because without the cause of American supremacy— growth and greatness as ends in themselves—the language of national solidarity and national purpose has evaporated. America has its own version of the imperial deep freeze—stuck in a history of past success and present inertia. The expansive success of the military-industrial complex of the 1950s with its corporate-managerial norms is now a frozen technocratic legacy blocking the historical imagination. Americans still measure themselves by the standards and values of the Greatest Generation and their boomer offspring. They measure economic and political success against an anomalous apex point of US power and prosperity, the 1950–1970 period. These acts of obedient traditionalism impart to "future-oriented" American culture a deadening conservative backwardness. The norms and expectations of midcentury US society have left two or three generations of younger America with a bland and belated dedication to replicating ways of life and myths of greatness whose economic base has been transformed by the last fifty years.

Just as Victorian ruling-class values long held sway over UK culture and politics, now a reverential view of American greatness cuts across classes and regions, locked in the amber of an Eisenhower-Kennedy era version of technical triumph over economic limits. The UK ruling-class ethos and the US managerial ethos are not identical. But they are both distillates of elite control, each stamped

by their respective superpower template. Victorian imperialism, as Perry Anderson observes, "created a powerful
'national' framework which in normal periods insensibly
mitigated social contradictions and at moments of crisis
transcended them altogether" (26). Class compromise, a
cardinal point of the Nairn-Anderson theses, takes a different shape in US mass society than it did in the Victorian Age. But the high noon of American hegemony and
Cold War consent culture welded US elites to well-paid
labor and the middle class. In addition, as C. Wright
Mills influentially argued in his account of the US
"power elites," the business class and the professionals
had common cause at midcentury. They formed a block
that Barbara and John Ehrenreich dubbed the "professional-managerial class." As Bernard Porter correctly notes,
US corporate technocrats were quite unlike British aristocrats in mores and style (126). But they occupied similar positions in a historical structure that emerged at a
similar point in what Arrighi calls the US-led cycle of
accumulation.[2]

The system of US class compromise formed in the
Cold War has shown remarkable staying power over the
last forty years of relative decline. But its bonds are wear-
ing down as the US enters its terminal crisis. Decline has
split the state/experts/minorities Democratic bloc from
the corporation/managers/white working-class Republican bloc. One side protects the regulatory state and the
other champions a freer market. The recent American
story of this intraclass split has been covered in specialist

books (Mizruchi). The working class has also been more and more untethered from the idea of shared American success. When elite and nonelite interests separate, and the pie shrinks, the possibility for a fundamental shake-up of class relations becomes more real. But so does the entrenchment of existing hierarchies. The picture is complex. British elites gained and maintained control of many institutions during the long downslope after 1900. As Richard Lachmann observes, that control gave the UK propertied class short-term advantages while blocking the kind of democratization that would have broadened prosperity. Brenner makes the same case about the US since the 1970s. Financialization protected the wealth of propertied elites who sought the deregulation of US markets. But it blocked the reinvestments that might have produced sustainable growth and expanded household incomes.

When class interests splinter in the age of decline, conservative visions of once and future greatness glue them back together. Culture wars pull nonelites to the right—a familiar truism of US electoral politics. It is rare though for mainstream political commentary to root this truism in the baseline problem of superpower nostalgia. Panning back to look at both UK and US trajectories over the last 150 years, it becomes clearer that the deteriorating consensus or lost center of American politics produced an identity crisis for citizens of all kinds. Political sentiments that once attached to America's manifest destiny—from the western frontier to the moon landing—have nowhere to go now but backward. No wonder mythic attachments rule over rational class interests.

The predictive value of Tom Nairn's line of analysis in *The Break-up of Britain* is especially vivid here. Fifty years into US decline, as the terminal crisis slowly settles in, the break-up of America seems more like political realism than dystopian fiction. American civic identity has been heavily vitiated by global power just as English nationalism once was. The US may be several stages behind actual devolutionary or secessionist movements. But the fault lines are there. The rigidifying divides of Red/Blue ideology and rural/urban politics in America—set alongside a working-class drift to the right and the retrenchment of white conservatism to its ethnic core—point to a fractured nation.

Comparative analysis suggests that the loss of hegemony as a galvanizing mission meant—for the UK, then for the US—the slow hollowing-out of nationalism itself. And an empty nationalism degrades into right populism. J. D . Vance's 2016 *Hillbilly Elegy* suggests that the rural working class in the US reached a similar crossroads. Underemployed and undereducated white voters have— as in the days of Thatcher—aligned with an insurgent right wing for cultural reasons stemming from lost status. In the face of national decline—or, better put, in the face of declinist thinking —working-class disaffection attaches to populism. The New Left developed an emotional and cultural vocabulary for this stubborn political pattern. Their work suggests that the US progressive movements need to forgo rational appeals to economic self-interest. Facts and policies do not move the needle. But national myth does. And as long as American national myth is rooted in declinist thinking, the needle points backward.

The surge of populist energy in the declinist era of the UK bears a strong resemblance to Trumpism now. Trumpism is both anti-state and anti-future, anti-elite and anti-globalist. It gains energy from nativism and racism, and it flares and flashes in many emotional forms—disaffection, despair, anxiety, rage, nostalgia—all of which can find cracks in the American political system. Britain's culture of decline puts the rightward drift of American politics into a fuller historical context, especially in light of the New Left's understanding that real economic and social losses attach to imaginary political causes. MAGA thinking and a deregulated economy work in tandem: real inequality stokes fantasies of loss and betrayal. Mainstream analysis of the MAGA phenomenon often centers on "left behind" white rural men. But the sense of lost greatness is a national problem, one that reverberates across gender, region, race, and class divides. It belongs to everyone who feels diminished in the face of rapid historical change.

Nairn and Hall identified the structure of feeling associated with rotted imperialism, a political sentiment rooted in the discourse of lost national supremacy.[3] Over time with real economic reversals, it shrinks into nativism. It carries paranoid thinking from hegemon culture into decline culture, where it festers. Richard Hofstadter's famous analysis of the "paranoid style" named the phenomenon as a matter of conservative US politics, but I think it's a deeper cultural substrate—a conservatism that afflicts American liberals, as it were. I would call it phobic hegemony. Phobic hegemony means the fear and anxiety generated by the anticipation of losing global power and privilege. Anxiety has always haunted American power: for those at the very top, change can only mean loss. Phobic hegemony was the dark underside of both Victorian equipoise and Cold War confidence. Paranoid style is not just a feature of midcentury American conservatism. It's a baked-in feature of superpower political culture.

Alas, it's also a feature of *ex*-superpower culture. It's not just a grotesque expression of Trump-era nationalism, in other words. Its roots run deeper. As real power ebbs, phobic hegemony gives political shape to the broad public anxieties about lost greatness. The high consent-conformity index of the early Cold War lives on as a symptom even when its political warrant has dissolved. The consensus politics of the McCarthy years, shaped by Red Scares and other racialized enemy discourses within and without, enshrined an "American way of life" that was both fragile and invincible. Such a culture cannot countenance dissent. As Stuart Hall notes, once "mesmerized by consensus," a society loses its ability to foster democratic debate *without* paranoia (Hall 23). Paranoia shapes declinism as a conservative force; it's the toxic residue of phobic hegemony. Under its baleful influence, all questions about American supremacy and national virtue are not honorable protest but sinister betrayal. Paranoia is the abscess that hegemony leaves under the skin of the Anglo-American body politic.

The parochial nativisms and white nationalisms operating under the cover of Trumpism within the Republican party echo the racist sentiments in UK politics to which Thatcher gave cover. These days, the reflex language of American supremacy is becoming more and more the property of a racial sect, white nationalists, derived from a racial caste, white citizens (Wilkerson). The new white nationalisms in the US are invented racist traditions. They are not natural expressions of "pioneer experience" nor emanations of so-called Lost Cause thinking from the Old South. Whatever their tin-pot iconographies say, the new white nationalists emerged in the declinist crucible. Their internet targeting of disaffiliated young white men was a conscious strategy conceived and executed by Steve Bannon with donor support from the Republican establishment. Bannon-Trump are the American symptom of declinism gone to rot, just as Enoch Powell was in the run-up to Thatcher. And as Pankaj Mishra rightly notes, the Murdoch media empire was there to support white nationalism in both epochs, on both sides of the Atlantic.[4]

When the language of lost greatness is not enough to stoke nativist anger, the language of black crime and lawlessness does the job. Stuart Hall and his colleagues established a significant and sharp connection point between the Thatcher and Trump eras: anti-Black police violence as a symptom of decline. It is no coincidence that the decline-and-dominance phase of US history since the 1970s corresponds to the war on drugs and the massive expansion of nonwhite incarceration. After decades of increasing inequality and relative decline, American elites have tacitly accepted a model of dominance and control rather than social consent.

The racist underpinnings of a new control society were predicted and identified by the British New Left fifty years ago during their epoch of national descent. Few commentators on police violence in the US now think as systemically and historically as did Hall and his team in *Policing the Crisis* when they connected racialized crime reportage to national decline: "We believe, then, that the nature of the reaction to 'mugging' can only be understood in terms of the way society—more especially, the ruling-class alliances, the state apparatuses and the media—responded to a deepening economic, political and social crisis" (306). Such arguments are coming into focus in America now, particularly as the links between scarcity, status anxiety, and white moral panic become more visible. Police violence in the Trump era has induced a broad and growing sector of the public to see the problem as one of social justice rather than law and order. Media commentary on urban crime seems to be breaking free of the old racist narratives, in part because Americans are coming to see the historical roots of police violence in slavery and Jim Crow.

Police violence is the domestic expression of the militarization that Arrighi identifies as one major hallmark of hegemons in free fall.[5] States that have in effect served as the world's self-appointed policemen end up militarizing their economic growth and their social norms. That is a structural problem of decline, exacerbated by the paranoid dimensions of declinism as a rhetoric of threat and loss. In America since the 1970s, propertied elites have felt decreasingly secure about their assets and their safety. Nonelites have become still less secure about theirs. Both of those feelings have justified the growing commitment to control society during the long downslope from Nixon to Trump.

The British New Left developed an early and cogent response to the class and racial dynamics of imperial decline. Their integrated model of the culture of contraction is invaluable for Americans thinking about the problems and possibilities in a society shaped by fading hegemony. But the New Left had diagnostic failings worth noting. Their intellectual movement has largely remained a dissenting, minority, and academic position within a UK society still drifting right, still circling lost greatness, still Brexiting. Looking back at the New Left thinkers, it can seem as if they believed that nothing ever changes fast enough or in the right direction. That a transformative workers' movement never arrived remained a frustrating conundrum. It's a curious blind spot for historians attuned to what Arno Mayer called the "persistence of the *ancien régime.*" In one sense their great strength—the attempt to understand one specific state and its national cultures—was also a limitation in thinking about the power of a long and *global* bourgeois-industrial revolution. That revolution may be a thing of the past in the UK, but it is still making its way through China and the Global South. In an integrated world system of societies and economies, capitalism continues to expand and renew itself. The socialist revolution, if it is to follow the globalization of an industrial and postindustrial middle-class, may still be a long way off. The old elites and oligarchical forms remain strong in both the UK and the US, and indeed across the developed world.

Meanwhile, the problem that haunted the New Left was the infection of the popular/democratic with the populist/authoritarian. It was a problem they could never solve in theory or in practice. Their brilliant diagnostics of declinist conservatism and their passionate affirmations of working-class struggle—definitive for the generation of E. P. Thompson and Raymond Williams—could not will into being a political transformation in the UK. The viability and vigor of bourgeois and traditional institutions seems to have caught them up short. The successful Tory union of elite leaders and nonelite voters—like the plutocratic-populist appeal of Trumpism today—is a difficult lock to pick. The social conservatism of the economically marginalized is now more an established fact than a political surprise. The right-wing coalitions of Thatcherism then, and Trumpism now, are a familiar feature of decline politics. But they are growing more radical in contemporary America. The British example, even as a lost opportunity, is vital for that reason. It points to the need for a direct and concerted intellectual disarmament of declinism, of the superpower nostalgia that is the cultural jet fuel of right populism. That project must be more than academic, more than a marginal, progressive, dissenting circle. The good news is that the history wars have already become a national conversation, so the arguments against freezing American life in the exclusive image of the founding fathers—or the Cold War technocrats—are already loose in the wild.

## NEW IDEAS FOR OLD COUNTRIES

In chapter 4, I will address the wider circle of culture and media beyond academic institutions. But since the matter of a history war is an educational one, I want first to address the problems and possibilities of cultural agency for humanists and historians. Let's return to the scene of the New Left as a university-based movement built to take on the turbulence of a nation in distress and decline. One key principle established by Perry Anderson in his essays of the 1960s is that ideas are themselves always subject to history. To think about the end of empire in the UK meant thinking within the limits set by the present conditions. Intellectuals may imagine seeing around the corner of history, but the horizon lines of the future are, in the end, inviolable. More precisely, a national culture formed by decades of imperialism cannot dismantle itself overnight.

In 1968, Anderson took stock of the arrested development of English ideas in "Components of the National Culture." The clotting of UK intellectual life in the face of a decelerating growth engine was, Anderson suggested, visible across all fields of knowledge. Anderson blasted the conservative orientation of the disciplines. For him, the failed modernization of British politics and British industry also meant the failed modernization of ideas themselves. Anderson's signature contribution was to criticize the status quo disciplines of his day. They showed their students a presentist, individualist, and economistic view of social relations and human values. That view was an undead leftover from the long liberal hegemony of Victorian ruling-class habits of thought. The intellectual class—and particularly the social scientists, Anderson observed—were thinking mostly about stable equilibria and individual actors. This produced two startling absences: a theory of historical change and a theory of collective action. Those two intellectual habits stripped the educated UK public of a working language for social change. It circumscribed the future. And it left the next generations languishing in the slough of declinist nostalgia.

The sweep of Anderson's survey is almost impossible to imagine reproducing for the American academic and cultural world, though Daniel Rodgers in *Age of Fracture* offers an inspired, synthetic intellectual history of the US from 1975 to 2001. The specialized silos and heterogeneity of the arts and sciences today, and the scale, diversity, and dynamism of American higher education, make such a thing hard to conceive, let alone undertake. It's very difficult to analyze the "present crisis" from within the crisis and to analyze the limit points of institutional thinking from within the institution. But here again the resonances between postwar UK universities and the present US universities are striking. The New Left project unfolded against the turbulent backdrop of students protesting against an undemocratic system, a stale curriculum, and high costs. Student protest movements were of course widespread in the 1960s, but the UK faced a particular crisis sharpened by the culture of contraction. How to modernize the institutional form and the disciplinary content of an educational system designed to produce elites for an empire that no longer needed governing? Both aspects of this problem bear on the US university system today. At the level of institutional form and access, US higher education faces a serious debt crisis, a defunded faculty, and a raft of unanswered questions about teaching students whose futures no longer bear out Eisenhower-era presumptions about economic growth, the demand for American expertise, or the long-term security of professional-managerial careers.

And, more to the point, Anderson's address to the common structure among the UK university disciplines bears intriguingly on the current life of knowledge within American higher education. US universities have been shifting further and further toward the dissolution of a once vital compact between basic science and applied research, between the liberal arts and instrumentalized vocational training. Anderson's analysis seems apt as a take on academic and public-policy conversations in the US today. Critical vocabularies for collective action or social transformation are generally thin compared to piecemeal, empirical methods designed to describe but not to question the status quo. What Anderson identified as a presentist, individualist, and economistic view of social relations and human values does dominate the university. As Daniel Rodgers notes, for example, the dominant strain of Rawlsian liberalism, the one that holds the US center left together over the last two generations, envisions a "more equal society" using "the most individualistic and economistic of premises" (185). Schematically we might say that traditionalism and empiricism defined the house style of both gentrified British academia and technocratic US academia.[6]

Indeed, as the intellectual wing of a long-successful industrial hegemon, US academia was organized in the post–World War II period for brilliant technical description and sturdy replication of the social and political status quo. Science and technology were routinely revolutionized, but social formations and cultural forms were to be replicated and preserved. Like all the other industries developed in those postwar decades of the American summer, US higher education has lingered in the shadow of its Cold War incarnation for a long time. The Innovation University has not adapted to the Autumn of the System. Incredible technical achievements continue, but students and the general public are decreasingly informed about the past and about the world beyond America. Many sectors of the public reflexively think of musicology or art history as boutique disciplines, yet accord almost instant authority to the historically shallow world pictures produced by messy data coming out of quantitative disciplines such as sociology or economics. The point here is not to rehash the usual lament of humanists in a society organized around instrumental reason. The point is to understand which parts of Anderson's original analysis stem specifically from the crisis of a UK society (an ex-empire) in decline and can therefore be borrowed to comprehend US society (an ex-hegemon) as it enters a comparable stage of decline.

Here too the picture is complex. The "curse of success" has kept US universities in a somewhat traditionalist frame of mind, reinforcing the categories of knowledge and forms of thought that were crystallized in the post–World War II era. Perhaps the disciplines remain to some degree locked in a nostalgic embrace of Cold War institutions and norms, but the US university system is much larger, more well-resourced, and more wide-ranging than the elite UK system that Perry Anderson was describing in the 1960s. US universities operate within a more dynamic economy and a more variegated media and cultural system. They are already more diverse than were the postwar UK universities. Despite an austere fifty-year diet of withdrawn state resources, American universities still have a critical mass of vibrant humanistic and social-scientific research ready to rise to the occasion of generating new ideas for life in a "second place nation."

Many US institutions are already actively committed to the project of reframing US history for the future, without supremacist underpinnings. The history wars reflect a serious open contest over the meaning and future of American greatness and American decline. And in fact the intellectual legacies of the British New Left are significant resources in that effort. E. P. Thompson helped inspire the core work of Cedric Robinson on racial capitalism and the work of many others who are challenging the racial predicates of English, history, philosophy, and classics. Lauren Berlant's *Cruel Optimism*, like other influential studies of national sentiment, picks up on foundational concepts from Raymond Williams, including "structures of feeling." Williams's influence can be felt all over contemporary cultural studies, especially in projects addressing the economics and sociology of care in the welfare state. Williams anticipated the need to reinvent welfare as a humane matter of tradition, belonging, and community rather than a form of statist overreach or a partisan idiolect of the left. Hall's *Policing the Crisis* finds a contemporary analogue in Stuart Schrader's *Badges without Borders*. Both connect a fading hegemon's aggressive posture overseas to the militarization of its domestic police. Hall and his colleagues produced a thick description of "control society" as a feature of a declinist panic in the UK, and their model is a suggestive precursor for control society research by digital and media scholars such as Alexander Galloway.

These quick examples highlight various attempts to break the intellectual habits formed in universities during the Cold War. In fact, the humanities and interpretive social sciences have advanced, for decades now, a stinging critique of US power and American exceptionalism. The apparent tension there—intellectuals replicate the forms of Cold War technocracy while opposing its values—points to an immediate problem that this book aims to address.[7] University and media elites have failed to develop a broad, compelling, and public narrative of American history that candidly acknowledges the costs of US supremacy without alienating popular nationalist sentiment altogether. The core of the problem has been, I think, that the center-left establishment refuses to cede the language of US supremacy while the progressive left and the cultural left refuse to accept nationalism altogether.

The center speaks the old language of American hegemony but still loses the emotional war for gut patriotism to the right. Meanwhile, the left refuses altogether the language of national sentiment. This the British New Left historians did not do. Chilled by the dangers of right populism, they nonetheless remained stalwart in their appreciation of popular pastimes, everyday life, and even national tradition. Stuart Hall saw decades ago that left and Labour political sides needed to take seriously the traditions, pleasures, and sentiments of the people. Elite dismissals of gut patriotism—a temptation for progressives in Trump's America—were alien to the British New Left. Their goal was to understand the beliefs and values of their fellow citizens, not to shame or mock the populist mind. Bad ideas—racism, nativism, authoritarianism—were to be displaced by better ones. Because they valued historical comprehension over political condescension, their work remains a beacon for us.

To be sure, Hall and his colleagues wondered whether it would be possible to separate UK nationalism from British imperialism. Paul Gilroy, viewing the landscape in 2011, allowed that UK nationalism might never be "purged of its racialized contents" (111).[8] Why seek to salvage a national culture if racist and colonialist thinking are written into its political DNA? It is fair to ask the same question now about America. What does American nationalism mean without supremacy and its racist and colonialist entailments? But replacements for the nation are hard to find even in a so-called global era. The nation-state is the operating scale for most significant collective action (taxes and services, laws, wars, policies and budgets). The nation-state holds the material resources. It also holds the symbolic resources. It persists because of its mythic appeal to origins and ends. This cuts to the quick of declinist nostalgia. Decline raises core existential anxieties rooted in the fear of death, of limits, of finitude. Growth and optimism have been particularly powerful organizing concepts for the American belonging. Hegemony exacerbated the tendency of Americans to invest in a romantic myth of a youthful, expansive nation. The myths of boundless growth and permanent supremacy are hard to give up when they have come to signify the health, future, hope, and solidarity of the people.

For this reason, American greatness has remained a rallying point. It still holds the liberal center. Barack Obama, though a self-avowed fan of Reinhold Niebuhr's indelible warning about the pitfalls of US power, had to disavow relative decline in order to appeal to the electorate. No US president since Carter has dared truly to address the meaning or trajectory of a gradual American twilight. The national self-image does not tolerate anything less than first place on the world stage.

When liberals and moderates stand aghast at the power of Trump and MAGA, they often seem to miss the long-term consequences of American hegemony. The fact of American supremacy in 1950 engendered a desire for American supremacy that lives on and on, gathering cultural force even as it loses its economic foundation. The language of national supremacy appeals not just to rural whites cut adrift from factory, farm, and mining jobs, but to middle-class white voters who feel the psychic sting of persistent status anxiety, consumer debt, and lost social mobility. The Trump voting bloc—like the Thatcher bloc—included a large number of affluent and propertied voters, mostly white and disproportionately male (Bhambra). The desire for US supremacy underlies both white nationalism and right populism, that's a given. But it also underlies the inability of the political center to comprehend the problem and to rewrite the language of American destiny.

The US political center has a blind spot when it comes to national greatness, believing that the rhetoric and even the practice of US supremacy can be maintained for political appeal and economic advantage without harming a progressive and democratizing agenda. The reflex invocation of American superiority seems harmless, habitual, and anodyne, but it is not. Not anymore. The left too rapidly gives up the nation; the center too stubbornly clings to greatness. But both can be rallied to look past these blind spots if we can decommission declinist thinking. Now that the US is a second-place nation, it becomes possible to pry American nationalism apart from global supremacy. It becomes possible to redefine a collective destiny without manifest destiny and to rebuild an emotionally resonant, widely democratic patriotism that is not predicated on violent exceptionalism.

The New Left project's most significant and timely legacy is a method for approaching national culture that includes political and media elites, the entertainment and arts system, and the academic world. Culture, broadly speaking, is information and interpretation—facts and stories. The university stores most of the facts. The media system controls most of the stories. The knowledge components of US national culture—universities—are just

starting to break free of the Cold War's decisive orientation to social equilibrium and American exceptionalism.
But what about the fantasy and entertainment apparatus
of America as it rounds the corner from signal to terminal
crisis? In the next chapter, I consider the emerging narratives and symbols that are changing the meaning of US
culture in and for the age of limits.

## 4 AMERICAN CULTURE IN THE AGE OF LIMITS

In Britain, the culture of decline is a vestige of the twentieth century. But in the US, decline is still taking shape. The 2020s will be the decisive period for American culture in the age of limits. What can generate a sense of shared mission or common purpose in the US if not the old vision of global supremacy and endless growth? Claiming to be number one while riddled with anxiety about being number two is not going to be a strategic or competitive advantage. What if, instead of chasing lost greatness, American culture figured out a way to face the slow losses and the past failures, building a future from there? The risk of staying in a declinist mindset is evident from the UK, which remains mired in what Paul Gilroy has called postimperial melancholy. Melancholy takes over, according to Freud, when a lost object has not been mourned. The melancholic person—or, in this case, nation—cannot name or face the lost object. As a result, the melancholic simply orbits symptomatically around

its missing center. Gilroy suggests that UK citizens have
so far failed to mourn their lost empire. To clear "the
debris of their broken narcissism," he writes, means
learning to acknowledge "the brutalities of colonial rule
enacted in their name and to their benefit" (99). In a
moving counterpart to Gilroy, Amy Kaplan in 2009
described imperial melancholy in America with a similarly tempered yet optimistic sense of purpose: "It may be
possible to relinquish and even mourn for imperial
America and to embrace an untold future" (31). For the
US to mourn its power means becoming conscious of its
history and its blind spots. Many humanities disciplines
have been pursuing that goal for years, but the debate
over the half-life of American exceptionalism is now a
serious public and political contest.

The problem of declinism in America is not just the
problem of UK-style melancholy. Americans have to
contend with a mixed inheritance, one part melancholic
attachment to lost power, one part blinding optimism
about the possibility that power has not truly, or perma-
nently, been lost. Because of this contradiction, American culture endlessly orbits the question of its status and
power, rather than simply acknowledging that its hegemony is real and enormous, but impermanent, and already
fading.

Because American optimism is tinged with anxiety,
melancholic stories of autumn and twilight, diminishment and collapse—or of Greatness Restored—always
seem to command center stage. And although the

trajectory of decline is different in the US than it was the UK, our version of superpower nostalgia often follows British precedent. British stories and ideas have been shaping popular notions of imperial glory (lost or found) for generations. They are embedded in the English media that have spread around the globe. As Fareed Zakaria notes: "Britain has arguably been the most successful exporter of its culture in human history. We speak today of the American dream, but before it there was an 'English way of life'" (187).

There is in other words a funny paradox in American culture. It began in revolt against British sovereignty and defined itself for generations against UK ruling-class values of crown, empire, and tradition. And yet in the Golden Age of Hollywood, on the run-up to American hegemony, the ideology of empire reentered the American bloodstream, adapted for mass society and a technocratic state. The medieval term *translatio imperii*, which once described the divine succession of emperors, later named the westward drift of power. It mutated into a doctrine of manifest destiny for aspirational American settlers (Stephanson). Back in the midcentury, Americans were able to believe that the sun set over the Pacific, casting its final golden beams on the new media capital of the twentieth century, Los Angeles. The historical bedrock of Hollywood genres has long been the rise and fall of empires, the romance of conquest, and frontier adventure. Americans learned to imagine their place in the Cold War world through a Hollywood vision that was neo-Victorian. When

I hear people complain about the recycled superhero franchises and numbing sequel factories of today's Hollywood, I am doubly surprised. First because the studio system was built on formula and repetition. And second because so many of the formulae, especially for action films, were recycled from nineteenth-century action-hero narratives. Westerns retold the frontier conflicts of British conquest across the globe. Victorian myths like *Dracula*, *Sherlock Holmes*, *The Invisible Man*, *The War of the Worlds,* and *Treasure Island* drove early Hollywood. The American media empire of the midcentury wasn't just making sequels. It *was* a sequel.

## SEQUEL CULTURE

Classic Hollywood extended and adapted late-Victorian Britain's remarkable storytelling industry. Those two dream factories spoke English to the world. They codified a distinct set of narrative templates for a global audience (Joshi). The economic and symbolic advantages of that export trade are still accruing. "The film is to America," wrote an anonymous reviewer in the *London Morning Post* in 1926, "what the flag once was to Britain."[1] In the 1980s, Stuart Hall marveled: "Empires come and go. But the imagery of the British Empire seems destined to go on forever. The imperial flag has been hauled down in a hundred different corners of the globe. But it is still flying in the collective unconscious" (*Hard Road* 68). Still true, forty years later.

Rudyard Kipling's infamous charge to Americans in 1899 to "take up the White Man's burden" has long been tagged as a racist antique, but the core message of a relay from British to American supremacy remains a subtext in popular culture on both sides of the North Atlantic. Many of the virulently patriotic languages of American adventurism—both as a superpower and perhaps even more toxically as an ex-superpower—have origins in the swashbuckling language of the Victorian Great Game. The old British myths of global dominance crystallized forms of racial enmity—the Yellow Peril, the Red Scare, the Muslim Threat—that have shaped not just geopolitics but US storytelling conventions into the Cold War era and beyond. Old myths of Anglo-Saxon Christian virtue cinch British empire to American hegemony by moralizing the history of conquest, extraction, and racial capitalism. They celebrate, however tacitly, the superior capacity of Anglo-American white men to invent, to produce, to manage, and to govern both nature and other peoples.

Victorian and neo-Victorian genres have deposited habits of thought that reinforce both the luck and the virtue of history's white victors. White supremacy and Anglo-American rule became entwined in the long schoolroom of empire and embedded in US popular culture. But those narrative formulae have an obverse side. As thrillers, they also tend to underscore the vulnerability of the Anglo-American core to invasion and degeneration. Consider Britain's star franchises over the last century, from the archetypal vampire (Dracula) and detective

(Sherlock Holmes) of the 1890s to the fantasy kingdoms (Tolkien's trilogy) and fantasy geopolitics (Fleming's *Bond* novels) of the midcentury, all the way to the magical boy-hero Harry Potter of the 1990s. These are all stories centered on archaic social forms—the blood-sucking aristocracy in Stoker, the degenerating empire in Conan Doyle, medieval allegory in Tolkien, the global derring-do of British adventure in Fleming, and the tony charms of the Victorian public school in Rowling. The threads of successful Anglo mass-cultural stories converge on themes of older social hierarchies propped up by an embattled empire, of social order threatened by corrupt villains but protected by unlikely heroes. These British myths recycle the glamour of global rule along with the fear of national degeneration.

British myths of freedom share a historical silhouette with American myths of freedom. Both were cemented in place at times when these twin hegemons presented themselves as the vanguards of modernity and the champions of human liberty. The abiding mythic core of liberal imperialism in both its Victorian British and Cold War American incarnations tells of a white, Western, or even specifically WASP proclivity for free markets and fair play, for heroic discovery and overseas rule (Green). As Priyamvada Gopal notes, this specific Anglo-American fantasy views freedom as a gift to, from, and for the English-speaking peoples, and as a "franchise generously extended to peoples across the globe" (3). The core paradox—freedom imposed by force—can never quite be stabilized in theory or practice. It therefore requires mythic expression. Its contradictions keep generating new stories. It has produced an entire Anglophone popular culture centered on what we might call the triune mythology of weak states, strong markets, and free individuals.

The mythology of the weak state/strong hero shapes many genres in the romantic adventure tradition of both UK and US popular culture. In them, heroes solve problems and save people because the impersonal, inefficient, or hostile state cannot.[2] The weak state myth is one of the most influential British ideas transmitted in the US bloodstream, and it helped perpetuate the notion—even through the high Keynesian decades 1940–1970—that individuals and markets are better than collectives or states at making choices. That brand of individualist thinking is a Victorian relic. UK and US liberal hegemons established for their educated elites the possibility of believing that—of living as if—the free individual was the ultimate social actor. The fantasy of autonomous selfhood conceals within its most intimate weave a deep attachment to an aristocratic notion of privilege and superiority. Its Americanized, modernized version—the self-made (white) man—is the locus of conservative political desire. It operates as a pseudopopulist fantasy of solo achievement, inalienable social distinction, and hard-won wealth.

The twin fantasy of self-regulating subjects and self-regulating markets is the imaginative bedrock of weak-state mythology. In reality, of course, the UK and the US always mixed free trade and protectionist policies. Preaching trade liberalism while protecting economic advantage propelled the US to great global wealth, just as it had done for the British Empire. What is lost in the crisis of national decline is precisely that myth of free trade, the mythic self-image of the economic hegemon styled flatteringly as a crusader for global laissez-faire. Trumpism marks the spot where that self-image crashed. The isolationist and protectionist turn of the Trump movement exposes American weakness while trumpeting strength.

At the cultural level, of course, the rhetoric of Trumpism is an attempt to recycle Reagan—already a recursive exercise in nostalgia *for* nostalgia (for Anglo-American rule). The power sources of America on the downslope—finance and the military—were mystified and celebrated in 1980s zeitgeist films like *Wall Street* and *Top Gun*. But the Reagan era mostly rehearsed its attachments to Western power through its nostalgia for the Edwardian- and Eisenhower-era good life. Raj-revival films of 1980s Hollywood expressed the Anglophilic strain of this sentiment. *Back to the Future*, revisiting Cold War social forms, literalized the domestic strain. Superpower nostalgia still pours into those same fantasy vessels now, circling the halcyon Edwardian and Eisenhower days. Consider *Downton Abbey* and *Mad Men*, two popular TV shows that took off during the uncertain years after the 2008 crash. Elite audiences warmed themselves to stories about the last confident epochs of Western power, led by

British aristocrats and American technocrats. *Downton* turned on the question of whether *rentier* wealth could be sustained in the face of decline (answer: yes, for one last generation, with imported capital from an American wife). *Mad Men* dramatized the fragile creation of wealth in an industrial American economy rapidly shifting toward the media-entertainment-military-service-financial sectors (Goodlad). Uneasy at times, but ultimately reassuring, these shows revisit the glory days of English-speaking elites. They offer the conservative lure of a glamorized past that is nonetheless compromised by the elites' benighted views of race, class, and gender. Such fantasies flatter progressives while installing a backward drift of historical desire. Surely *Mad Men*, which ended its run in 2015, sheds a revealing light on the primal 1950s' pleasures associated with Donald Trump the taboo breaker—steaks, golf, white certainties, and a violently seigneurial sense of heterosexual privilege. All popular culture may cannibalize and mash up the past, but in the UK and the US, the apex stages of national supremacy have a particularly tenacious hold on the half-buried political desires that live on in their aftermath.

## DECADENCE TO DYSTOPIA

Even at their peak, superpower cultures are haunted by phobic and lurid fantasies about the loss of power. Decay within and enemies at the gate are the perennial specters. They drive degeneration plots and invasion scenarios, providing the jolt to what Susan Sontag called "the imagination of disaster." Sixty years earlier, Joseph Conrad called it "the defensive mandate of a menaced society." And ex-superpowers are even more menaced than the liberal hegemons that Sontag and Conrad were describing. Can it be a coincidence that the British and American dream factories each produced its own characteristic undead specter during the slide into terminal decline? The vampire myth codified by Bram Stoker in the 1890s anticipates the zombie myth, which has steadily gained traction in America since the 1970s. The vampire, a moldering aristocrat, points to the dead hand of the old ruling class in Britain. The zombie, an automaton of mindless appetite, points to the decadence of mass consumer society. Both take root in the popular imagination of societies falling off peak. Both describe societies that consume themselves, prey to their own excess.

America the undead hegemon is both a vampire and a zombie: it is dilapidated yet powerful (Harman). The contradiction of declinism—once *and* future greatness—comes to gothic life in the bloody geopolitical fables of our times, these tales of resurrection. The zombie craze in post-2000 US culture is one face of a widening market share for dystopian and apocalyptic fiction (Hicks, Hurley). Apocalyptic visions are not the stuff of sensationalized military, sexual, ecological, and nuclear disaster genres, but a taken-for-granted realist element in the literary fiction of Cormac McCarthy, Colson Whitehead, Ling Ma, and many others. As Dan Sinykin observes, tales of "neoliberal apocalypse" track neatly to the long downturn.

Meanwhile, the fables of invasion that once flowed out of British publishing houses and American studios are now starting to share significant cultural space with Asian productions.[3] Adam Tooze reports that Chinese popular culture of the last fifteen to twenty years has featured "a massive diet of TV and film offerings preoccupied with the question of the rise and fall of the great powers" (252). The notion that the future is now made in Seoul and Shanghai surely helped pave the way for the US-market success of Liu Cixin, whose *Three-Body Problem* seemed to be everywhere in 2015, and of Bong Joon-ho, whose 2019 gem *Parasite* won the Best Picture Oscar and the Palme D'Or at Cannes. *Parasite* and *Three-Body Problem* both exploit the shock value of the home invasion plot, the first scaled to the domestic zone of privacy, the second to the planetary zone of sovereignty. Bong updates the underlying symbols of the classic western (cowboys and Indians clashing over the possession and dispossession of land) to startling, satisfying effect in the violent denouement of his film. The western will never be the same. Meanwhile, *Three-Body Problem* trades on the core fear that animated H. G. Wells's *War of the Worlds* back in the 1890s (or Philip K. Dick's *The Man in the High Castle* in the 1960s). Alien invasion plots map flexibly onto colonial history, with the reader's point of view swapping between identification with the invaders and the invaded. Such blockbusters mark the switch points between great powers—the shifting tectonics of British, American, and Asian cycles of accumulation. At such times, the wheels of history grind heavily, layering the destinies of old and new hegemons into the thriller plot of invasion and defense. For Liu, as for Wells and Dick, the imaginative breakthrough—the conceit of a successful alternative world—has its taproot sunk deep into the uncertainty of contemporary geopolitics. It turns the flux of the great powers—their contingent past, their uncertain future—into sensational plots.[4]

## THE CLOSED FRONTIER

It's been 130 years since the US Census Bureau announced the closing of the West and Frederick Jackson Turner responded with his frontier thesis. But the American frontier concept has been kept alive ever since by powerful narratives of expansion and growth. Forty-two states became fifty. The US map extended far across the Pacific. Haiti came under the US flag in 1915. The Space Age rebooted manifest destiny. Global adventurism in the Cold War reopened the expansionist mindset of American politics. Even cyberspace seems to have rekindled the colonizing and enterprising imagination of the US state and US firms. American culture reproduces for every new generation the idea that American society is a future-oriented, boundless entity. Frontier thinking persists here just as the ancien régime persisted in European history.

But even the extended life of America as an evergreen and symbolic Frontierland is changing after several decades of relative economic decline. The closed frontier—as opposed to the closing frontier—will bring a different kind of imaginary horizon home to Americans. Four distinctive aspects of the present mark the 2020s as the turning point between frontier futurism and the culture of contraction. First, and most important, there is the hard limit of climate change. Climate change marks not just the demographic limit of the US frontier (1890) or the terrestrial limits of Euro-American exploration and settlement (1912, at the South Pole), but the sudden and disastrous realization of finite space. The planetary limits of dominated nature have been reached, even breached. Second, the transfer of capitalist dynamism across the Pacific marks a different kind of end to the five-hundred-year cycle of Westernization. The Eurocentric organization of foreign affairs since the Victorian age means that American people and policymakers view—are trained to view—Asian power as threatening. Third, the project of extraterrestrial travel and exploration has now passed from a nation-state project to a corporate and private enterprise. It is no longer Britain or America or China that is pushing the frontier open, but Virgin Galactic (UK), SpaceX (US), Blue Origin (US), Galactic Energy (China), i-Space (China), and Link-Space (China). The people's investment in their nation's expansive mission (the patriotism of the Apollo years) seems more and more like a relic of the twentieth century. Finally, the Trumpist fantasy of a walled America marks the end of the open frontier in a different but equally epochal way (Grandin). The expansive frontier of the US state—open and incorporative as a brawling multiracial settler colony in the nineteenth century and a geopolitical and technological juggernaut in the twentieth—may close itself off to new people and new growth.

It's not that US innovation and dynamism are dead. Far from it. Scientific and technological advances are boggling minds now just as they did in the time of Bell and Edison. But as the idea of endless US expansion hits a new set of real and symbolic limits, American culture starts to look more backward than forward. The pivot point is here. America needs new stories, not an endless run of paeans to national glory lost. America's destiny as the last great power was a powerful historical idea that grounded Cold War culture. Now it is a fading fantasy.

## MUSEUMS OF POWER

Superpower nostalgia deepened—as did the neoimperial call to arms—in the Bush II era. 9/11 exacerbated the aggressive defense of US power, while the 2008 crash exacerbated the anxious defense of elite American wealth. The protagonist of Mohsin Hamid's *The Reluctant Fundamentalist* (2007) captures the quickening of lost greatness in New York after 2001:

I had always thought of America as a nation that looked forward; for the first time I was struck by its determination to look back. Living in New York was suddenly like living in a film about the Second World War; I, a foreigner, found myself staring out at a set that ought to be viewed not in Technicolor but in grainy black and white. What your fellow countrymen longed for was unclear to me—a time of unquestioned dominance? of safety? of moral certainty? I did not know—but that they were scrambling to don the costumes of another era was apparent. (115)

Hamid shows us twenty-first-century Americans looking back wistfully at twentieth-century certainties—power, wealth, preeminence. That backward glance replicates the least productive elements of British declinism.

Hamid's novel captures the predicament of citizens estranged from the future by collective nostalgia. The quest for moral certainty has also estranged Americans from the national past. It encourages them to see history as a shrine of national virtue. But American history was a site of bloody struggle and messy contingency as well as considerable social progress.

In the years since 2001 and since Hamid's text, though, US supremacy is becoming a historical object more than a holy grail. The old military-industrial complex is slowly becoming the stuff of heritage. Back in the mid-twentieth century, historical tourism collected the memories of an agrarian, frontier, and preindustrial past. Colonial Williamsburg, Knott's Berry Farm, Greenfield Village—all of these pre-Disney sites of recreational Americana were in full swing by the 1950s. These days, and especially for Americans born after 1975 (two-thirds of the population), the Cold War concept of US industrial preeminence *is* an artifact. Steel mills and grain towers are becoming art lofts and climbing walls. Disused military bases and equipment are now tourist fodder. The world's best-selling pickup truck, the Ford F-150, is now assembled in a hybrid facility featuring the Ford Rouge Factory Tour. NASA tours in Houston, Cape Canaveral, and Huntsville present the US space program as historical narrative.

The US is capturing in institutional amber the means of production that once secured its wealth and preeminence. Britain too gradually shifted identity from world's workshop to museum culture. That process was well underway between the world wars and continued apace in the 1970s and 1980s. Of course the backward-looking orientation of decline culture can cut two ways. Postimperial melancholy can give way to something just as regressive, a stylized and fetishized view of the nation's past, kept under glass or molded into theme-park plastic. From Julian Barnes's satiric bite in *England, England* (1998) to Alex Niven's reading of Alton Towers in *New Model Island* (2019), the path of national self-caricature should alert us to one potential danger for America on the downslope. In the Thatcher era, a fierce debate broke out over the national heritage. In *On Living in an Old Country*, Patrick Wright described the elite capture of the historical imagination in Britain. Gentrified nostalgia for country houses presented "a highly selective image of British particularity…as the essential identity of the betrayed nation to which we must all return" (Wright 26).

Wright's analysis anticipates the viral spread of "betrayed nation" rhetoric in the contemporary US. That rhetoric almost always recycles the weak-state version of US history in which the real actors are heroic individuals (settlers, founding fathers, inventors, entrepreneurs). But are there alternatives to believing that America—whether understood as a republic of heroic men or as a colossus of capitalist expansion—has lost its essential identity in the era of relative economic decline? In the early 2020s, it would appear that the last redoubt of a redemptive strong-state narrative lies in what we might call the infrastructural imagination. Infrastructure feeds the center right a conservative vision of steel girders and concrete pylons framed against the big sky—an America that still builds things. But it also feeds the center left a vision of public works and democratic access—a state that can solve problems at a New Deal scale. Joe Biden's rallying cry for new infrastructure investment was unfiltered superpower nostalgia. In April 2021, he called his successful bill "unlike anything we've done since we built the Interstate Highway System and won the Space Race decades ago."

Biden's swashbuckling state embodies American might in steel and concrete, but it also delivers broadband and child care. It disengages US energy and purpose from global dominance and overseas expansion, bidding for the vanishing center of American political life. The infrastructural imagination has become a lively topic for humanities scholars, too (Guldi, Ho, Lieberman, Mattern, Rich, Robbins, Rubenstein). These scholars have largely seized on infrastructure to salvage the ideal of the welfare state in the face of its dismantling from Reagan through Clinton forward. As Janice Ho and Marc Stears have both noted, infrastructure rallies ordinary people to the humble, everyday state services that they need—train tracks, post offices, water lines—rather than to the global ambitions of old empires. Infrastructural nationalism can function as a transitional narrative to carry the US from morbid declinism toward productive life as an ex-superpower.

## DEINDUSTRIALIZING EVERYDAY LIFE

Nothing epitomizes the ethos of decline—or the age of limits—better than the rising prominence of "degrowth" as an economic program. Today's degrowth movement has its origins in 1970s ideas—E. F. Schumacher's *Small Is Beautiful* (1973) and Herman Daly's *Steady-State Economics* (1977), for example. Schumacher's book—subtitled "A Study of Economics as if People Mattered" was a bestseller. It marked the convergence of 1970s declinist thinking with early sustainability economics. Today, at the far end of the 1970–2020 declinist arc, the degrowth position associated with Kate Raworth has been gaining attention and (often younger) adherents. Raworth's proposal is that states should steer their economies into the sweet spot between what she calls the social foundation (decent standards of living for all) and the ecological ceiling (scientific limits to growth). With climate crises mounting, the call to thrive rather than grow has become more convincing (Booth, Kunkel, Pilling, Speth). Degrowth aims to cast off the holy grail of constant high growth. It aims to salvage prosperity, dynamism, and creativity from the expansionist logic of the old national capitalisms.

Whether Raworth's sweet spot can be achieved in the face of capitalism's drive for constant accumulation and boundless expansion—and in the countervailing face of the forces of secular stagnation—is a question for economists, or prophets. But its cultural significance is clear. It is the economic language designed to redeem the culture of contraction, to prepare Americans for the next stage of the long downturn. Economists and economic historians of all political stripes have been announcing the end of American (and European) high-growth economies for some time now (Brenner, Cowen, Gordon, Graeber, Piketty, Summers, Thiel).

In the face of many headwinds, the degrowth movement aims to makes an economic virtue out of a historical necessity. Elite consumers in the US have already followed suit, turning the deindustrialization of their economy into an opportunity to deindustrialize everyday life and decentralize commerce. Simplicity chic and artisanal production have swept everything from farmers markets to the new urbanism, from herbal healing to barefoot running, from Marie Kondo–style anti-materialism to the growing celebration of vocational tradecraft over professional education. The last twenty years have been a golden age for DIY creativity. The internet mutes the old mediating role played by corporate hierarchies, cultural gatekeepers, and the middleman industry. Consider the rise of fanfic and Soundcloud, blogs and vlogs, Ebay and Etsy. Internet commerce allows for a direct exchange between makers and buyers. It creates an immediate flow of art, ideas, goods, and services. Homemade clothing, recycled toiletries, tiny houses, and #vanlife: millennials and zoomers are busy lowering their household overhead. Contemporary American foodways make the trend more obvious still and echo the agrarian nostalgia of midcentury Britain. Composting communes, picklers and brewers, oyster ranches, urban gardens, vertical farms, organic marijuana plots, backyard chicken coops, foragers, freecyclers, and home beekeepers—such postindustrial back-to-the-land practices don't change the reality of modern mass agronomy at global scale. But they do mark an elite investment in the idea of pastoralism and sustainability as core principles for American domestic life. At the cultural level, they are a very serious expression of a longing for a better way of life in a deindustrializing nation that has hit the edge of a sick planet.[5]

Many of the social trends rapidly flagged in this account of post-peak American culture are, admittedly, elite and consumerist phenomena. In deindustrializing

Britain, the neo-pastoralisms of the decline decades featured a certain chic superficiality. Alex Niven's account of "British middlebrow and hipster" localism and pastoralism will ring some bells for American readers: "that strange blend of homespun craft, nu-folk music, austerity chic, organic food and autochthonous nationalism." (52). The danger of nativism that Niven flags in his analysis of millennial Englishness is the same one described by Paul Gilroy as Anglocentric "geo-piety" (114). What seem like innocuous claims to land and tradition, to foodways and folkways, can imply ethnically exclusive notions of belonging. Who belongs to the land is perhaps an even more fraught question in the US, given its indigenous and immigrant histories.

NEW PARTICULARISMS

Superpower cultures are metacultures. They absorb, manage, and integrate the content of other, more particular, more embodied, more bounded cultures. Holding the hegemonic center causes nations to develop an image of themselves as the neutral and technical edge of modernity. In a sense their culture is a gravitational core, the hub of the system. But it thereby becomes an empty core, leaching content, losing meaning. This feature of superpower culture once defined Victorian British and Cold War US liberalism. Britain's satellite cultures were, Tom Nairn observes "more easily summed up in typifying commonplaces" than England's own, which "lays hold of universalism via its imperial power, rather than suffer the partiality of stereotype" (293). Hegemon cultures were, at their peak, lands of form without content, built on vague value terms such as freedom and greatness. Their cultures were extendable insofar as they were emptied of specificity. In 1871, Matthew Arnold zeroed in on the problem:

> Freedom, like Industry, is a very good horse to ride—but to ride somewhere. You seem to think that you have only got to get on the back of your horse Freedom, of your horse Industry, and to ride away as hard as you can, to be sure of coming to the right destination. (344)

What Arnold called the anarchy of late-Victorian British culture grew out of the weak state/strong economy model. Market society had no organizing purpose beyond wealth—no wonder then that in the decades after Arnold's treatise, the new imperial mission filled the vacuum of collective meaning. Its successor hegemon, the US, likewise deferred real political struggle and generated social consent with a constantly expanding frontier. Both liberal hegemons also fostered an intellectual aversion to grand, utopian, or collective planning—a skepticism of strong-state action and a preference for negative liberty over positive freedoms. British empiricism and American pragmatism were the great expressions of liberal hegemony in the Anglophone world. In Arnold's terms, both nations grew by industry and empire, and so long as they did, they could ride horses without picking destinations. As Reinhold Niebuhr observed eighty years after Arnold, a great power can avoid existential political conflict and "vexatious issues of social justice" as long as its expansive phase lasts. But what happens, Arnold and Niebuhr wondered in their turn, to collective, national values when growth hits its limits? Greatness hid America's internal fault lines. Decline makes them gape.

Power, growth, and global influence made the Victorian UK and the Cold War US into civilizational managers of other cultures. What happened to English culture over the course of the twentieth century is now starting to happen to US culture. It is becoming more and more the restricted object of its own gaze rather than an expansive subject with investments in understanding the rest of the world. The society supports less and less robustly the study of non-Western languages and cultures, now that the area-studies funding model based on Cold War strategic interest has been withdrawn. The shrinking of US power brings with it the prospect of an unfortunate parochial turn, as the imperial giant collapses into a white dwarf. The racist dimensions of that collapse, the "movement away from universalism" in declining America, is the core subject of Emmanuel Todd's 2003 study *After the Empire* (Todd 109).

Once again, the British precedent defines a fork in the road ahead for US culture. Healthy particularism can devolve into narrow parochialism. When a culture's ability to self-universalize becomes subject to age and decay, a fine balance must be struck. Particularism means ceding the claim to speak for humanity, not ignoring the rest of the world. A de-exceptionalized American elite is now learning to think about world affairs in neutrally global rather than "late Western" terms. That means rethinking relations with Asia, with Islam, and with the Global South from outside the old paradigm of Euro-American primacy. The future of decline—the recovery and renewal of American culture—might allow Americans to look at the world *and* America afresh, from unaccustomed angles. "Throughout the twentieth century, the world at large was 'Americanized,'" Joseph Cleary has recently observed. "Now, America, often reluctantly, sometimes with furious backlash, is gradually being Asianized, South Americanized, Africanized and Europeanized, and otherwise transformed by its immigrant histories" (215). Particularized America is not "post-America," nor is it "little America." US strength, wealth, and dynamism do not depend on the export of American values as if they were universal human norms.

## NEW REALISMS

The dream factories of America grew out of the media-age technical revolutions of 1880–1920 (cheap print, cinema, photography, radio, gramophone). These technologies consolidated the culture industry so that the great mass of American citizens came to be, "more than anyone on Earth," immersed "in the virtuosic fantasies created and sold by show business" (Andersen 136). The entertainment empire was not just an export industry for American stories. It was a gigantic machinery for establishing fantasy versions of US supremacy. Commentators such as Neal Gabler and Jackson Lears have captured the idea that America arrived at its epoch of peak power armed with a massive apparatus for generating fantasies. Daniel Boorstin: "We risk being the first people in history to have been able to make their illusions so vivid, so persuasive, so 'realistic' that they can live in them" (240).

The entertainment empire prepared midcentury domestic audiences for global power. The popular culture of imperialism grew strong pumping out films organized around a fairly rote concept of white Western superiority. Those habits die hard, even on the downslope. Since the decline era began in the mid-1970s, from *Star Wars* and *Indiana Jones* to *The League of Extraordinary Gentlemen*, from *Superman* to *Avengers: Endgame*, two historical sources of mythic content have transfixed Hollywood: Victorian Britain and Cold War America. These two nations at peak power gave essential form to all the blockbuster genres. American superheroes crystallized into a durable archetype around 1940, just in time for the American Century. Now they crowd our screens, pumped-up and airborne transmitters of superpower nostalgia. Trump-era Hollywood also has a strong neo-Victorian nostalgic streak: *The Legend of Tarzan* (2016), *The Lost City of Z* (2016), *The Jungle Book* (2016), *Mowgli* (2018), *Doolittle* (2020), *The Invisible Man* (2020). All of these British genre films stoke the fantasy of a boundless and ageless America. Next on the big-budget docket for Disney? A *Peter Pan* reboot.

But US film—despite franchises that aspire to the name of "universes" or "multiverses"—has been losing its global dominance for decades. Even in the domestic entertainment market, the legacy media such as feature films have now been challenged by all kinds of new media, which are organized less and less around national myth-making. Neoclassic Hollywood films still retail superpower nostalgia and imperial fantasy. But the independent visual storytelling and short-form genres of the internet and small-town papers more often focus on stories about social collectives, common causes, and shared care. These are everyday realities of an American society bound to itself rather than a flailing nation in search of superheroes and strongmen. To put this another way, scripted fantasies leveled at high-gloss wish-fulfillment have become corporate artifacts because their time in the sun is passing.

A new realism of sustainable, collective, postsupremacy American life is starting to coalesce as decline culture matures. The last thirty years of American entertainment has brought a remarkable, concerted, and multimedia shift from the scripted to the real. From the memoir boom that kicked off in 1995–96 with the success of *The Liars' Club* and *Angela's Ashes* to the rise of reality TV programming (*Survivor* debuted in 2000), from the artistic and political vitality of documentary film to the ubiquity of YouTube's million-eyed gaze on domestic, intimate, and quotidian reality, new kinds of reality-based forms have displaced fantasy. The massively decentralized and expanded cultural media now use their vast skimming and recording power to make daily life available. It's an autoethnographic bonanza of everyday American eyes on everyday American lives. What David Shields called in 2010 the "lure and blur of the real" seems to be growing (5). That shift makes sense when we consider the received history of British literary culture during the Suez era of the 1950s and 1960s—the terminal crisis of British hegemony. There we find a marked rise of both autoethnography and neorealism in England.[6] Despite the reliable commercial appeal of romance genres and aristocratic settings, midcentury British writing was newly committed to representing ordinary life in direct observation. It is tempting to conceptualize those developments as features of a newly bounded national life, an inward and realist turn for a superpower learning to adjust the scale of national fantasy.

At the outset of this chapter I attempted to characterize declinist Hollywood as inclined to produce either dystopic reflections of lost greatness (zombies for a moldy superpower) or bloated spectacles of renewed greatness (superheroes for an evergreen superpower). But Hollywood is always canny about emerging narratives—it does not just recycle the residual ones. Despite the pressure of superpower nostalgia, the national myth factory of Hollywood has been rotating on its axis over the last decade.

It looks for opportunities to tell the stories that will resonate in a diverse society and in an ex-superpower. Take
for example, the shift in emphasis and sensibility from
*Avatar* (2009) to more recent space adventures. *Avatar* is
classic colonization-allegory sci-fi. It was framed by its
maker, James Cameron, as an update of such Anglo-
American myths as *Lawrence of Arabia* and *John Carter of
Mars*. It features the plot that Renato Rosaldo has memo-
rably called "imperialist nostalgia," in which the destroy-
ers and exploiters of colonized worlds express regret but
no fundamental challenge to their own power. *The Martian* (2015) is still a Hollywood crowd pleaser, but its
major themes are (a) the conservation of scarce resources
and (b) the fragility and alienness (not the romantic
bravery) of the white male explorer. Like other recent
space epics such as *Gravity* (2013) and *Arrival* (2016)—
both of which are woman-centered, *The Martian* turns
on interlocking plots of sustainability and of cooperation
with China rather than on aspirational American power
as the ultimate geopolitical referent.

Addressing the history of slavery and racial capitalism
became a preoccupation in US film during the years from
Obama to Trump. Hollywood worked in earnest—if not
always successfully—to undo the legacy of racist American "classics" such as *Birth of a Nation* (1915) and *Gone
with the Wind* (1939). Recent productions such as *12 Years
a Slave* (2013), *Harriet* (2019), and *Underground Railroad*
(TV series, 2021) have begun to displace not just the old

epics of anti-Black Hollywood but even the white-liberal-centered accounts of Black history such as the earnest *Glory* (1989), the execrable *Amistad* (1997), and the virtuous *Lincoln* (2012). Black genre films have been updating the usual formulae, including the horror movie (*Get Out* [2017]), the western (*The Harder They Fall* [2021]), and the superhero movie (*Black Panther* [2018]). *Watchmen* (2019) was a genre TV series that revised the white vigilante plot and centered viewers' attention on the Tulsa massacre of one hundred years earlier—a horrifying moment in the history of racist violence.

Black-centered revenge and action plots (which might also include 2012's *Django Unchained*) revise a dominant Hollywood formula in which white male individuals take the law into their own hands to save home, self, family, or the social order. Westerns and crime films often turn on this figure of the beset white renegade, casting him as the necessarily violent yet moral center of a world where society and nature are both inimical to his autonomy. At times this figure seems like the distillate of the by-now legendary left-behind Trump voter, prepared to do violence in order to reassert his social status and his property claims. The vigilante is a recurrent figure of the American imaginary, one that rose to center stage in the downslope decade of the 1970s, as embodied by Charles Bronson (*Death Wish*, 1974). The vigilante has been revived consistently—for example in Michael Douglas's *Falling Down* (1993) and Clint Eastwood's *Gran Torino* (2008).

Beset white manhood is perhaps the defining plot of declinist America, particularly when it imagines a sudden, violent purgation of social disorder.

Vigilantes and superheroes occupy different sectors of the genre continuum, but they share the fundamental commitment to what I called weak-state mythology. In both genres, meaningful social action—including violent action—belongs to individuals, not the state. Even with a Black or Asian (*Shang-Chi*, 2021) superhero in place, it is difficult to budge that founding principle of the genre system.

But two recent, successful films starring Frances McDormand—*Three Billboards Outside Ebbing, Missouri* (2017) and *Nomadland* (2020)—offer clues to a different kind of plot for the age of limits. The protagonist of the first hails from a town called Ebbing and in the second from a town called Empire. Ebbing Empire: the theme of American decline is woven in from the start. These two hometowns, one dedicated to farming, one to mining, represent the economic plight of rural workers. After traumatic violence and economic dislocation, both movies reimagine the western journey of the disenfranchised, disaffected heroine. In both, the protagonist is seeking to recreate home and family. In *Three Billboards*, she is seeking vengeance, but she doesn't get it. The two core anxieties of American decline—lost security and lost prosperity—drive these films. Failed economic and political safety nets (including the police) are a given at the raw, rural frontiers of race and class. These two visions of the tattered American dream are directed by non-USnative directors (Martin McDonagh is from Britain; Chloé Zhao is from China—the past and future hegemons again!). Their plots end up offering what audiences can take as a sharp but subtle counterpoint to white male vigilante films—all the same dislocations and losses, but with woman-centered stories aimed at survival and acceptance. Without a cathartic fantasy of getting back what has been lost, these films operate as transitional myths pointing the way out of the MAGA-and-melancholia quagmire.

National myths and tropes persist in these new films, particularly the open concept of the western journey/ road trip. National myths persist, but their meanings change under the pressure of history. Academic critics of American power probably cannot fully demystify the nation as the symbolic center of government power and collective action. But they can participate in the redefinition of its meaning. Myth-busting American exceptionalism is only a first step. The society needs replacement languages of national meaning in the wake of the old exceptionalism. To break the melancholic allure of lost greatness, those languages will need to go beyond declinist thinking. And they will need to have visceral bite, affective depth, and affiliative power.

## FEELING LIKE A SOCIETY

American exceptionalist thinking will persist even in the multipolar world of the twenty-first century. After all, as

Brexit reminds us, British exceptionalism has long survived the eclipse of UK hegemony. One of the most consequential subtleties I discovered in researching midcentury UK culture was the "second-order universalism" that accompanied national decline and to some degree managed the loss of hegemony. "To absorb the lost privileges of imperial centrality," I argued, certain English intellectuals sought to restore "to England its historical privileges as the archetype of modern industry and empire, and therefore the archetype of a new age of post-industrial, post-imperial national life. The archetypal turn of thought—in which England is somehow the 'most typical' modern society because it is the *oldest* modern society—retains a second-order universalism" (191). That formula gave the ex-superpower UK, and its presumed English cultural core, a unique claim to depth and integrity. Bernard Crick captured the point much more succinctly in 1959 when he observed that Britons had abandoned their aspirations to be the "Rome of power" but remained invested in the project of being the "Athens of example" (qtd in Ian Hall 6). Second-order universalism may help Americans break the habit of speaking for the planet or the species, but it probably will not break the habit of viewing America as a chosen nation, a model society, the archetypal democracy.

Americans have been trained by a long run at the economic top to believe that they live in not just a good society, or even a great society, but the best society ever. This brittle patriotism will surely survive in a new form even as America's global aspirations shrink. Perhaps it is a necessary fiction for the sake of the present social order. The central question of this book is whether a popular and resonant language of national renewal can carry America past the declinist horizon of the last fifty years. Since the 1970s, the binary formula we are still dominant/we are in decline has left little space for a vital third term: revival through contraction. To break the impasse between growth culture and decline culture may require a purposeful transition from what I would call first-order universalism (America sets the pattern for all cultures) to second-order universalism (America sets the pattern for itself, but in a way that is distinctive and archetypal). That way of thinking decouples national dynamism from the aggressive export of US values and norms.

The beacon pointing the way to a smaller, saner, wiser America was lit in the early Cold War by Niebuhr's *Irony of American History* (1952). Niebuhr updated and Americanized the case made against UK expansionism by J. A. Hobson's *Imperialism* (1902) fifty years earlier. Niebuhr assessed the likely costs of Cold War hegemony for US culture and politics. Both Hobson and Niebuhr carved out a language of renewal by posing national integrity against the moral and social entropy of empire. They saw the future of the retrenching UK and US states not as contracted but as *concentrated*, and thereby improved. Charles Maier offers a more recent and temperate version of the point: "As the British and Dutch have learned, and as the Americans shall eventually have to as well, despite

the letdown, there can be a rewarding civic existence
once the hegemonic or imperial hour has passed" (77).

## HISTORICAL LITERACY IN AN AGE OF LIMITS

Mainstream declinists often imagine voluntary self-
correction as the solution to US decline. The right blames
the moral decay of a permissive welfare society. The left
blames the political decay of a neoliberal plutocratic society. In the face of these narratives, it is no wonder that
the public debate is filled with voluntarist ideas destined
to become policy impasses. Concerned citizens are told
to "come together," to "heal our politics," fix gridlock,
defuse partisanship, rebuild manufacturing, reform institutions. These exhortations to moral improvement, political compromise, and economic revitalization cannot
change the course of global capitalism. The material process of relative decline is slow and inevitable, and many
of its determining factors are happening on a planetary
scale outside the moral or political control of US citizens
and institutions.

On the other hand, while it is not easy to alter fundamental matters of belief and identity woven into the
mental habits of American supremacy, it is at least possible. And this is why the current history wars matter.
Americans are struggling now, often antagonistically, to
redefine their nation. The public reckoning with race and
empire that Paul Gilroy once described as the antidote to

postimperial melancholy is surely happening on both sides of the Atlantic. The statues of Cecil Rhodes and Robert E. Lee are falling. Those symbolic acts are a form of insurgent public history. But, as Pankaj Mishra points out, the "removal of memorials to slave-traders is likely only to deepen the culture wars if it is not accompanied by an extensive rewriting of the Anglo-American history and economics curriculum" ("Flailing" 14). Historical literacy as a matter of K–12 education and wide civic participation—not just of the higher education curriculum—is the only path forward that will keep the history wars from stalling out in the stark binary that asks students to demonize or to lionize American institutions. The resolution of the history wars depends on finding a shared language of national experience and national purpose, one that is not flooded with declinist panic or compensatory fantasies of privileged belonging restricted to white citizens and their consecrated property. The resolution of the history wars matters—it is anything but academic. The meaning of the American past sets the predicates for future state actions and for the distribution of resources.

But history and the humanities are starving for resources just when we need them most. Inside the corporate research university, and ever since the austerities that kicked off in the 1970s, the drift of ideas is toward instrumental knowledge. The quest for the efficient delivery of usable, useful data has shaped the intellectual life of higher education in a time of declared austerity. Despite the conspicuous expansion of facilities, programs, administrators, and tuition bills, public and private universities shifted resources away from basic research in the arts and sciences. Intellectual innovation now refers almost entirely to quick solutions to immediate problems. When all the knowledge produced comes preapplied and all the questions come prevetted on grant applications, no breakthrough discoveries should be expected in the arts or the sciences.

The status quo is reproduced by the self-fulfilling prophecies of strategic plans driven by scarcity, forced into the impossible delivery of big ideas on a short clock. The current dispensation of universities underfunds what declining America needs most: basic research and development, sustained knowledge of cultures and languages outside America/English, and a deep, critical understanding of American and global history (Lye, Newfield, and Vernon). Working through the national past is a university-wide—indeed a society-wide—project. It is slow, expensive, controversial, and absolutely necessary. The status quo is also reproduced when the historical humanities—the only place left where American students are asked to think about the meaning of the past—are marginalized and disaggregated from the sciences and professions.

No doubt it seems rather predictable, perhaps even self-interested, for a university humanist to urge the revitalization of posthegemony America by investing in … the university humanities. But the call to comprehend

American society's place in history is made urgent by the tectonic shifts in America's status as a shrinking super-power. And the question of the nation's meaning or common purpose cannot be solved by technical and practical solutions alone.

The work of the public humanities now is to inspire readers, students, and citizens to think of the past as not given but made. Americans lack, but desperately want, a new definition of freedom that does not reduce to toxic individualism. They want a new set of stories that can signify American purpose beyond global supremacy. Decline has been an American obsession since the Puri-tans—a ghost story about lost integrity, diminished greatness, abandoned promises. The unfinished business of making America now depends on remembering some-thing better than world conquest and fading dominance. It depends on telling the story of American democracy again. Better ideas, Stuart Hall said, to replace bad ones. It's not magic.

No matter what the future holds, Americans need to demand a robust reintegration of technical and historical knowledge, of STEM, business, the professions, and the humanities. Consider the contextual force of the most famous statement we have about the disintegration of scientific and cultural knowledge, C. P. Snow's *The Two Cultures* (1959). Snow wanted to modernize British edu-cation, replacing the old ruling-class concept of classical learning with more technical and scientific training. Now, in the US of the 2020s, the poles of value are reversed. We must insist on historical literacy as the indispensable goal of modern humanistic education. Victorian ruling-class values held on too long in the UK, blocking the path to technological literacy. In the US the situation is parallel yet inverted: Cold War technocratic values have held on too long, blocking the path to civic engagement and historical literacy. Snow grasped that the problem lay in the growing fissure between technology and culture. He reflected brilliantly on the startling parallels linking Venetian and British power in their seasons of triumph and in their seasons of descent:

> Like us, [the Venetians] had once been fabulously lucky. They had become rich, as we did, by accident…They knew, just as clearly as we know, that the current of history had begun to flow against them. Many of them gave their minds to working out ways to keep going. It would have meant breaking the pattern into which they had crystallised. They were fond of the pattern, just as we are fond of ours. They never found the will to break it. (42)

It is hard to imagine a better commentary on the American present. Luck and power have frozen American thinking into a pattern. Many are fond of that pattern, but it belongs to the past.

## ACKNOWLEDGMENTS

I would like to thank Aaron Bartels-Swindells, Beth Blum, Matti Bunzl, Antoinette Burton, Max Cavitch, Joe Cleary, Jay Cushing, Maud Ellmann, Jim English, Jonathan Esty, Andrea Goulet, Heather Hicks, Seo Hee Im, Brittney Joyce, Peter Kalliney, Suvir Kaul, Eilis Lombard, Ania Loomba, Zack Lesser, Andy Lewis, Colleen Lye, Cliff Mak, Catherine Mallon, John Marx, Caroline McKusick, Graham McPhee, Alex Millen, Rivky Mondal, Nasser Mufti, John Plotz, Kelly Rich, Elias Rodriques, Gayle Rogers, Leon Sachs, Tony Salah, Paul Saint-Amour, Zach Samalin, Max Saunders, Claire Seiler, Jonah Siegel, Faith Wilson Stein, Michael Szalay, Joe Valente, Rob Waldeck, Callie Ward, Sarah Wasserman, Sam Waterman, Phil Wegner, Erica Wetter, Laura Winkiel, Chi-ming Yang, and Molly Young for invaluable help, insights, and encouragement.

# BIBLIOGRAPHY

Abu-Lughod, Janet L. *Before European Hegemony*. Oxford, 1989.

Acemoglu, Daron, and James A. Robinson. *Why Nations Fail.* Crown, 2012.

Andersen, Kurt. *Fantasyland*. Random, 2017.

Anderson, Perry. "Dégringolade." *London Review of Books* 26.17 (2 September 2004).

———. *English Questions*. London: Verso, 1992.

———. *The H-Word: The Peripeteia of Hegemony*. London: Verso, 2017.

Applebaum, Binyamin. *The Economists' Hour.* Little, Brown, 2019.

Arnold, Matthew. *Culture and Anarchy*. Penguin, 2018.

Arrighi, Giovanni. *The Long Twentieth Century.* Verso, 1994.

Baldwin, James. *The Price of the Ticket.* St. Martin's, 1985.

Barnett, Anthony. *The Lure of Greatness.* Unbound, 2017.

Baym, Nina. "Melodramas of Beset Manhood." *American Quarterly* 33.2: 123–139.

Bennett, William John. *The De-Valuing of America.* Simon & Schuster, 1992.

Berlant, Lauren. *Cruel Optimism.* Duke, 2011.

Berman, Morris. *Dark Ages America.* Norton, 2006.

Bernstein, George L. *The Myth of Decline.* Pimlico, 2004.

Bhambra, Gurminder K. "Brexit, Trump and 'Methodological Whiteness.'" *British Journal of Sociology* 68 (2017): 214–231.

Bin Wong, Roy. *China Transformed.* Cornell, 1997.

Boorstin, Daniel J. *The Image* (1962). Knopf, 2012.

Booth, Douglas E. *Hooked on Growth.* Rowman, 2004.

Bork, Robert H. *Slouching towards Gomorrah.* Harper, 1996.

Brennan, Timothy. "The Empire's New Clothes," *Critical Inquiry* 29.2 (2003): 337–367.

Brenner, Robert. *The Economics of Global Turbulence.* Verso, 2006.

———. "What's Good for Goldman Sachs Is Good for America: The Origins of the Current Crisis." (April 2009). http://escholarship.org/uc/item/0sg0782h.

Brill, Steven. *Tailspin.* Knopf, 2018.

Brzezinski, Zbigniew. "The Dilemma of the Last Sovereign." *American Interest* (Autumn 2005).

Burton, Antoinette. *The Trouble with Empire.* Oxford, 2015.

Calleo, David P. *Beyond American Hegemony.* Basic Books, 1987.

Campanella, Edoardo and Marta Dassù. *Anglo Nostalgia.* Hurst & Company, 2019.

Cannadine, David. *Ornamentalism: How the British Saw Their Empire*. Oxford, 2001.

Chetty, Raj, et al. "The Fading American Dream." *Science* 356 (2017): 398–406.

Chuh, Kandace. *The Difference Aesthetics Makes*. Duke, 2019.

Cleary, Joe. *The Irish Expatriate Novel in Late Capitalist Globalization*. Cambridge, 2021.

Cowen, Tyler. *The Great Stagnation*. Dutton, 2011.

Dalio, Ray. *Principles for Dealing with the Changing World Order*. Avid, 2021.

Daly, Herman. *Steady-State Economics* (1977). Island Press, 1991.

Davis, Mike. *Late Victorian Holocausts*. Verso, 2001.

Desai, Radhika. *Geopolitical Economy*. Pluto, 2013.

Diamond, Jared. *Collapse: How Societies Choose to Fail or Succeed*. Penguin, 2005.

Douthat, Ross. *The Decadent Society*. Avid, 2020.

Ehrenreich, John and Barbara. "The Professional-Managerial Class." *Radical America*. 11 (1977).

Elkins, Caroline. *Imperial Reckoning*. Henry Holt, 2005.

Esty, Jed. *A Shrinking Island*. Prinsceton, 2004.

Ferguson, Niall. *Colossus*. Penguin, 2004.

———. *Empire*. Basic Books, 2002.

Frank, Andre Gunder. *ReOrient*. California, 1998.

Friedberg, Aaron L. *The Weary Titan*. Princeton, 1988.

Fukuyama, Francis. *The End of History and the Last Man* (1992). Free Press, 2006.

———. *Identity*. Farrar, 2018.

Gabler, Neal. *Life: The Movie*. Vintage, 1998.

Getachew, Adom. *Worldmaking After Empire*. Princeton, 2019.

Gilroy, Paul. *Postcolonial Melancholia*. Columbia, 2005.

Goldberg, Michelle. "The Darkness Where the Future Should Be." *New York Times* (24 January 2020).

Goodlad, Lauren M. E. *The Victorian Geopolitical Aesthetic*. Oxford, 2015.

Gopal, Priyamvada. *Insurgent Empire*. Verso, 2019.

Gordon, Robert. *The Rise and Fall of American Growth*. Princeton, 2016.

Gore, Al. *The Assault on Reason*. Penguin, 2007.

Graeber, David and David Wengrow. *The Dawn of Everything*. Farrar, 2021.

Grandin, Greg. *The End of the Myth*. Metropolitan, 2019.

Green, Martin. *Dreams of Adventure, Deeds of Empire*. Marlboro Books, 1979.

Grieveson, Lee. *Cinema and the Wealth of Nations*. California, 2018.

Gross, Daniel. *Better, Stronger, Faster: The Myth of American Decline*. Free Press, 2012.

Guldi, Jo. *Roads to Power: Britain Invents the Infrastructure State*. Harvard, 2012.

Hacker, Jacob and Paul Pierson. *American Amnesia*. Simon & Schuster, 2016.

Hall, Catherine, Nicholas Draper, Keith McClelland, Katie Donington, Rachel Lang. *Legacies of British Slave-Ownership: Colonial Slavery and the Formation of Victorian Britain*. Cambridge, 2014.

Hall, Ian. *Dilemmas of Decline.* California, 2012.

Hall, Stuart. "Authoritarian Populism." *New Left Review* 151 (1985): 115–124.

———. *The Hard Road to Renewal: Thatcherism and the Crisis of the Left* (1988). Verso, 2021.

———. "The Local and the Global: Globalization and Ethnicity." In *Culture, Globalization, and the World-System*, ed. Anthony D. King. SUNY, 1991.

Hall, Stuart, and Chas Critcher, Tony Jefferson, John Clarke, Brian Roberts. *Policing the Crisis.* Macmillan, 1978.

Hamid, Mohsin. *The Reluctant Fundamentalist.* Penguin, 2008.

Hannah-Jones, Nikole, Caitlin Roper, Ilena Silverman, and Jake Silverstein, eds. *The 1619 Project.* One World, 2021.

Harari, Yuval Noah. *Sapiens.* Signal, 2014.

Harman, Chris. *Zombie Capitalism.* Haymarket, 2010.

Harootunian, Harry. *The Empire's New Clothes.* Prickly Paradigm, 2004.

Harvey, David. *The Limits to Capital.* Verso, 2018.

Hayes, Christopher. *Twilight of the Elites.* Crown, 2012.

Hensley, Nathan. *Forms of Empire.* Oxford, 2016.

Hicks, Heather J. *The Post-Apocalyptic Novel in the Twenty-First Century.* Palgrave, 2016.

Ho, Janice. "The Colonial State and Transnational Welfare during the 1930s Depression," in *The History of 1930s British Literature*, eds. Benjamin Kohlmann and Matthew Taunton. Cambridge, 2019.

Hobson, J. A. *Imperialism: A Study* (1902). Cosimo Classics, 2005.

Hu, Jane. "Typical Japanese: Kazuo Ishiguro and the Asian Anglophone Historical Novel." *Modern Fiction Studies* 67.1 (2021): 123–148.

Hubbard, Glenn and Tim Kane. *Balance: The Economics of Great Powers from Ancient Rome to Modern America.* Simon & Schuster, 2013.

Huntington, Samuel. "The Clash of Civilizations?" *Foreign Affairs* 72 (1993): 22–49.

Hurley, Jessica. *Infrastructures of Apocalypse.* Minnesota, 2020.

Hutchins, Francis G. *The Illusion of Permanence.* Princeton, 1967.

Ikenberry, G. John. *Liberal Leviathan.* Princeton, 2012.

Jameson, Fredric. "Future City." *New Left Review* 21 (2003): 65–79.

Jasanoff, Maya. "Misremembering the British Empire." *New Yorker* (26 October 2020).

Jendrysik, Mark Stephen. *Modern Jeremiahs.* Lexington, 2008.

Johnson, Chalmers. *The Sorrows of Empire.* Henry Holt, 2004.

Joshi, Priya. *In Another Country.* Columbia, 2002.

Kagan, Robert. "Not Fade Away: The Myth of American Decline." *New Republic.* (11 January 2012).

Kaplan, Amy. "Imperial Melancholy in America." *Raritan* 28.3 (2009): 13–31.

Kaplan, Robert D. *The Revenge of Geography.* Random, 2012.

Kennedy, Paul. *The Rise and Fall of the Great Powers.* Knopf, 1987.

Keohane, Robert. *After Hegemony.* Princeton, 1984.

Krugman, Paul. *The Great Unraveling.* Norton, 2003.

Kruse, Kevin M. and Julian E. Zelizer. *Fault Lines.* Norton, 2019.

Kunkel, Benjamin. *Utopia or Bust.* Verso, 2014.

Lachmann, Richard. *First Class Passengers on a Sinking Ship.* Verso, 2020.

Lasch, Christopher. *The Culture of Narcissism* (1979). Norton, 2018.

Lears, Jackson. *Fables of Abundance.* Basic Books, 1994.

Le Carré, John. *A Small Town in Germany* (1968). Pocket Books, 2002.

Lieberman, Jennifer L. *Power Lines.* MIT Press, 2017.

Luce, Edward. *Time to Start Thinking: America in the Age of Descent.* Grove, 2012.

Lye, Collen, Christopher Newfield and James Vernon. "Humanists and the Public University." *Representations* 116.1 (2011): 1–18.

Madrick, Jeffrey. *The End of Affluence.* Random, 1995.

Maier, Charles S. *Among Empires.* Harvard, 2006.

Mann, Michael. *Incoherent Empire.* Verso, 2003.

Martin, Will. "The US Could Lose Its Crown as the World's Most Powerful Economy as Soon as Next Year." *Business Insider* (January 10, 2019).

Marx, John. *The Modernist Novel and the Decline of Empire.* Cambridge, 2005.

Mathy, Jean-Philippe. *Melancholy Politics.* Penn State, 2011.

Mattern, Shannon. "Infrastructural Tourism." *Places Journal* (2013).

McCann, Sean and Michael Szalay. "Do You Believe in Magic? Literary Thinking after the New Left." *Yale Journal of Criticism,* 18.2 (2005), 435–468.

McClintock, Anne. *Imperial Leather.* Routledge, 1995.

McCoy, Alfred. "Fatal Florescence: Europe's Decolonization and America's Decline" in McCoy et al., p. 3–39.

McCoy, Alfred, Josep M. Fradera, and Stephen Jacobson. *Endless Empire.* Wisconsin, 2012.

Mishra, Pankaj. *Bland Fanatics.* Farrar Straus Giroux, 2020.
———. "Flailing States." *London Review of Books* 42.14 (16 July 2020).

Mizruchi, Mark S. *The Fracturing of the American Corporate Elite.* Harvard, 2013.

Morefield, Jeanne. *Empires without Imperialism.* Oxford, 2014.

*Munich Security Report 2020.* Munich Security Conference Foundation. https://securityconference.org/en/publications/munich-security-report-2020/

Murphy, Cullen. *Are We Rome?* Houghton, 2007.

Nairn, Tom. *The Break-up of Britain.* New Left Books, 1977.

Niebuhr, Reinhold. *The Irony of American History* (1952). Chicago, 2008.

Niven, Alex. *New Model Island.* Repeater, 2019.

Olson, Mancur. *The Rise and Decline of Nation.* Yale, 1982.

O'Toole, Fintan. *Heroic Failure: Brexit and the Politics of Pain.* Apollo, 2018.

Piketty, Thomas. *Capital in the Twenty-First Century*. Trans. Arthur Goldhammer. Harvard, 2014.

Pilling, David. *The Growth Delusion*. Crown, 2018.

Pomeranz, Kenneth. *The Great Divergence*. Princeton, 2000.

Porter, Bernard. *Empire and Superempire*. Yale, 2006.

Puri, Samir. *The Shadows of Empire*. Pegasus, 2021.

Raworth, Kate. *Doughnut Economics*. Chelsea Green, 2017.

Rich, Kelly. *States of Repair*. Forthcoming, Oxford, 2022.

Robbins, Bruce. *Upward Mobility and the Common Good*. Princeton, 2007.

Rodgers, Daniel T. *Age of Fracture*. Belknap/Harvard, 2011.

Rosaldo, Renato. *Culture and Truth*. Beacon Press, 1993.

Rubenstein, Michael. *Public Works*. Notre Dame, 2010.

Santiago-Valles, Kelvin. "The Fin de Siècles of Great Britain and the United States" in McCoy et al., 182–190.

Satia, Priya. *Time's Monster: How History Makes History*. Belknap/Harvard UP, 2020.

Schrader, Stuart. *Badges Without Borders*. California, 2019.

Schumacher, E. F. *Small Is Beautiful* (1973). Harper, 2010.

Shields, David. *Reality Hunger*. Knopf, 2010

Sinykin, Dan. *American Literature and the Long Downturn*. Oxford, 2020.

Snow, C. P. *The Two Cultures and the Scientific Revolution* (1959). Cambridge, 1961.

Song, Min Hyoung. *Strange Future*. Duke, 2005.

Sorkin, Aaron. "We Just Decided To." *The Newsroom*, season 1, episode 1. HBO, 2012.

Speth, James Gustave. *America the Possible*. Yale, 2012.

Stears, Marc. *Out of the Ordinary*. Harvard, 2021.

Stephanson, Anders. *Manifest Destiny*. Hill and Wang, 1995.

Straus, William and Neil Howe. *The Fourth Turning*. Broadway, 1997.

Streeck, Wolfgang. *How Will Capitalism End?* Verso, 2016.

Summers, Lawrence. "The Age of Secular Stagnation." *Foreign Affairs* (February 2016).

Tainter, Joseph. *The Collapse of Complex Societies*. Cambridge, 1988.

Tharoor, Shashi. *Inglorious Empire*. Hurst, 2017.

Thiel, Peter (with Blake Masters). *Zero to One*. Crown, 2014.

Todd, Emmanuel. *After the Empire: The Breakdown of the American Order*, trans. C. Jon Delogu. Columbia, 2003.

Tooze, Adam. *Crashed*. Penguin, 2018.

Turchin, Peter. *Ages of Discord*. Beresta, 2016.

Vance, J. D. *Hillbilly Elegy*. Harper, 2016.

Vernon, James. "When Stuart Hall Was White." *Public Books* (23 January 2017).

Wallerstein, Immanuel. *The Decline of American Power*. New Press, 2003.

———. *The Modern World-System*. Academic Press, 1974.

Ward, Stuart and Astrid Rasch. *Embers of Empire in Brexit Britain*. Bloomsbury, 2019.

Wegner, Philip E. *Life Between Two Deaths, 1989–2001*. Duke, 2009.

Wiener, Martin. *English Culture and the Decline of the Industrial Spirit*. Cambridge, 2004.

Wilkerson, Isabel. *Caste: The Origins of Our Discontents.* Random, 2020.

Wood, Ellen Meiksins. *Empire of Capital.* Verso, 2003.

Wright, Patrick. *On Living in an Old Country* (1985). Oxford, 2009.

Wynter, Sylvia. "The Ceremony Must Be Found: After Humanism." *Boundary II* 12:3 & 13:1 (1984): 19–70.

Zakaria, Fareed. *The Post-American World: Release 2.0.* Norton, 2011.

# NOTES

1. There was a left-liberal variant of moral critique to explain Carter-era malaise, as in Christopher Lasch's *Culture of Narcissism* (1979).

2. In retrospect, Fukuyama's view underestimated the fierce antagonisms centered on race, ethnicity, and religious identity that have persisted inside and outside the West (a blind spot he addresses in his 2018 book, *Identity*).

3. Min Hyoung Song looks back at the 1990s as a time when "the future became a place of national decline"(1). In the US, Song suggests, anxiety about decline was driven by "alien invasion [nonwhite immigration], the misery of poor urban blacks, and the declining fortunes of a white middle class" (19).

4. Contradictory beliefs are embedded in American culture. They limit the political and rational choices voters and citizens make. Culture limits policy progress. On this point, the Victorian sage John Ruskin understood the order of operations: "The history of every people ought to be written with less regard to the events of which their government was the agent, than to the disposition of which it was the sign" (qtd in Wiener

99). As America becomes a number-two nation, and then a number-three nation, new dispositions can be understood and described. More important, they can be changed, in a contest of ideas, in a debate—public and principled, fervent and even fierce—about what American destiny was, and is.

5. Lachmann's *First Class Passengers on a Sinking Ship* deserves special mention for its brilliantly capacious and systematic reading of imperial decline—chiefly Dutch, British, and American—over centuries. Lachmann offers a worthy sociological counter to Arrighi's *Long Twentieth Century*. His book also presents a rare combination of genuinely systematic and materialist thinking that is nonetheless invested in a voluntarist or "can-do" conception of what causes or fixes national decline.

6. Likewise, decline in the UK meant "a gradual running down of the great industries of the first industrial revolution, and a failure to wholeheartedly develop new industries" (Wiener 151).

7. There are different measures for global share of wealth and productivity, all of them inexact statistical models, but the two most commonly used are GGP and PPP. By PPP (purchasing power parity), China has already surpassed the US. It has gone from roughly 5% to roughly 20% of world economy share since the 1980s. The US has declined from roughly 25% to 15% in that same forty-year run (Sources: IMF, World Bank). By GGP (global gross product), projections vary over the next decade, with some believing China will surpass America in 2021, some in 2031.

8. "We are," writes Samir Puri, "in the first empire-free millennium in world history since ancient times, but the world remains in the throes of a great imperial hangover" (1).

9. Consider that the organizers of the 2020 Munich Security Conference set "Westlessness" as the event's theme. They registered their concern about a creaking NATO alliance, rising illiberal and autocratic trends in developed nations, and the general "decay of the Western project" (*Munich* 5).

CHAPTER 2

1. My analysis relies on Perry Anderson's useful definition of hegemony: the "outward expansion of the internal hegemony of a dominant social class, unleashing the energies of its rise to power beyond its state boundaries in the creation of an international system capable of securing the acquiescence of weaker states and classes, by claiming to represent universal interests" (*H-Word* 145).

2. Of course the problem is a general one, not just an Anglo or American one: Pankaj Mishra has observed that backlash violence against ethnic and religious minorities often stems from intense global competition. Mishra cites Arjun Appadurai's formula: "Minorities are the major site for displacing the anxieties of many states about their own minority or marginality (real or imagined)" (*Bland* 40).

CHAPTER 3

1. The full extension of Nairn's logic into the present is evident in Alex Niven's *New Model Island,* a contemporary polemic that proposes letting the concept of England go altogether. Niven's inventive regionalist scheme for the "break-up of England" cuts to the core of the problem. Britain signifies a nostalgia for lost greatness. England signifies an empty core incubating class and racial exclusion. Niven suggests that the society would survive better unfettered from both.

2. Bruce Robbins observes that aristocratic norms shape the meaning of "upward mobility" in many societies and literary traditions, so that the UK was not alone in confronting ruling-class anachronisms from within a modern welfare state (138). Meanwhile, ruling-class social advantage in the UK was partially transformed into professional expertise, a process that intersected with the highest phase of British soft power during the late Victorian and Edwardian period (Marx, *Decline*).

Members of the US expert class in the Cold War also understood their place as knowers, explainers, and problem definers
for global humanity. The era of decline in both the US and UK
undermines the social prestige and economic toehold of elite
professionals. Andrew Gamble's *Britain in Decline* notes that
1960s British society featured attacks not just on the bureau-
cracy and the unions, but also on science and the professions.
Gamble's analysis neatly anticipates the recent "twilight of the
experts" argument advanced here in the US by, for example, Al
Gore and Chris Hayes. Four years before Trump, Hayes pre-
sciently described the recent "cycle of populism, anti-elite
revolt, and oligarchic retrenchment" in the US (45).

3. There are relevant discourses of decline in many European countries, including in the second most retrenched ex-
empire, France. A survey of "Le Déclinisme" would feature
works by Pascal Bruckner and Nicolas Baverez. The general
pattern or discourse has been diagnosed aptly by Jean-Philippe
Mathy in his book on *Melancholy Thought*.

4. Murdoch's media outlets backed both Thatcher and
Trump. Both relied, as Mishra notes, on "an Australian media
tycoon almost as committed to a politics and culture of xeno-
phobia as his father, a stalwart of White Australia policy" (207).

5. Kelvin Santiago-Valles argues that the "British fin de siècle's panoptic and biopolitical mechanisms...have been resur-
rected, systematized, and implemented more brutally during
the US fin de siècle" (189). He cites the carceral state, the war
on drugs, three strikes laws, the war on terror, and homeland
security as part of an end-of-empire control society in both the
Victorian UK and the US after Nixon.

6. One part of this story is already familiar from Edward
Said's *Orientalism* (1978), which, like the work of the British
New Left, unfolded during the Gramsci boom of the 1970s.
Said argued that both humanistic and area-studies work in the

Cold War US was remarkably continuous with an older tradition of Eurocentric thinking about nonwestern societies.

7. Sean McCann and Michael Szalay offer a bracing discussion of the limits of "cultural struggle," that is, of intellectuals attempting to establish political agency through control of what C. Wright Mills called the cultural apparatus (439–441). It is striking that Mills's strong model of cultural agency, developed in the 1960s, anticipates and overlaps significantly with the work of Stuart Hall among others on the British New Left. It is just as striking, as McCann and Szalay suggest, that the cultural left in the US ended up more and more inside the technocratic elite model, living as well-compensated experts within the expanding postwar university. But now the larger framework of declining institutional support has brought that pattern to a crisis point.

8. Alex Niven believes neither British nor English nationalism can be functional, let alone progressive. Niven's solution is to go small (but not fetishistic) by reviving regionalism and urbanism. Paul Gilroy's solution is to go big (but not universalist) by championing an antiracist humanism. In calling for a better humanism, Gilroy extends a powerful tradition of anticolonial thinking that now includes Sylvia Wynter and Kandice Chuh. Gilroy's version is geared to disrupt "liberal, Cold War, and exclusionary humanisms"—precisely the ones that carried the Victorian imperial project across the Atlantic and into the Cold War (xvi).

CHAPTER 4

1. Lee Grieveson cites this anonymous piece in his indispensable *Cinema and the Wealth of Nations*. Grieveson summarizes the case: "Movies began to operate as the avant-garde for the spread of US commodity culture and capital across the world system" (6).

2. From the liberal British phase to the neoliberal American phase, such tales champion heroes over policies. They ignore the failures of free-market fundamentalism. Pankaj Mishra has been surgical and synthetic in capturing the Anglo-American myth of free markets. Hacker and Pierson describe the corresponding general amnesia about the state's role in delivering public goods.

3. Michelle Goldberg (citing Neal Stephenson) offers a recent versions of the idea that Western science fiction is running out of creative fuel, losing imaginative touch with the future.

4. Asian-American films with trans-Pacific plots are renewing other key Hollywood genres that still have life left in them: the rom-com (*Crazy Rich Asians*) and the family drama of migration (*The Farewell*). Jane Hu offers a synthetic new account of "generic Asianness"and its mediation of Anglophone narrative traditions against the backdrop of shifting global power (127).

5. There is a serious national identity significance to food. Beef production and consumption, for example, have defined Anglo-American settler colonialism and cultural imperialism from the iconic British Beefeaters to the global American hamburger. Wanton approaches to cattle ranching made the English-speaking world the land of the cow in all the arable spaces from Sydney to Winnipeg, Cincinnati to Johannesburg (Belich). But now the trends are reversing themselves in the face of climate change. This trend, too, tracks to the long downslope from the 1970s to now. On a per capita consumption basis, the US reached "peak beef" in 1979 and "peak meat" in 2004.

6. Inward-facing tourism and autoethnographic writing were major signs of contraction culture in the UK during the 1930s, '40s, and '50s (Esty).